About *Abundant Life*

Hank Lazer's *Deathwatch for my Father* (2004) changed my life, giving me access to grieving through poetry, using others' words as well as my own, tracked in diary form. For decades, he has been my guide in spirit and in sound, gathering simplicity across years of poetic and zen practice. I am grateful for this selection from his work of the last quarter century, the way it records one heart-mind, moment after moment, always in the present, yet becoming history in its accretions. Word by word he ties—and unravels—the knots (and nots) of existence. By the end each word feels luminous, empty in the Buddhist sense. We're left with a substantial, and wise, book by a marvelous, humane, poet.

—Susan Schultz

Hank Lazer's *Abundant Life: New and Selected Poems* is a book of books, a Golgonooza of dozens of notebooks. Lazer's poems are a daily practice whether of Jewish prayer, Zen meditation, early morning contemplation, or just plain poetry making— the active sense of rebalancing, setting himself and his readers to rights. Joining his thought we join the family: we become intimates with his grandmothers and uncle. The deathwatch elegies for his father and mother, deft and warm but unsentimental, frame the collection like pillars. Lazer is a man of words inspired by the words and music of others; his great gift is to receive. The poems skirt and skim Heidegger and Levinas, quote Creeley and Lyn Hejinian, are inspired by Monk and Coltrane, by kabbalah and Dogen, but also the prayer notes of his late Uncle Stan and rediscovered 1970's letters from his grandfather Chaim who anguished over war and peace. Inspired by both Genesis and Zen practice, Lazer is in love with beginnings. The poems originate from handwritten notebooks and range in form from abstract improvisational shape-writing, to tight homages to Creeley, to freely sprawling pages, to left margin stanzas. Always though there is a scent of mind renewing itself, a mind responsive to the immediate moment— but reflecting on the whole

thinking / is the real / dancing its way / inward

and the continuity of that mind as it responds to current events over the past twenty-four years is a steady marvel at the center of a massive swirl of stars, abundant life indeed.

—Rodger Kamenetz

ABUNDANT LIFE

ABUNDANT LIFE

New & Selected Poems

Hank Lazer

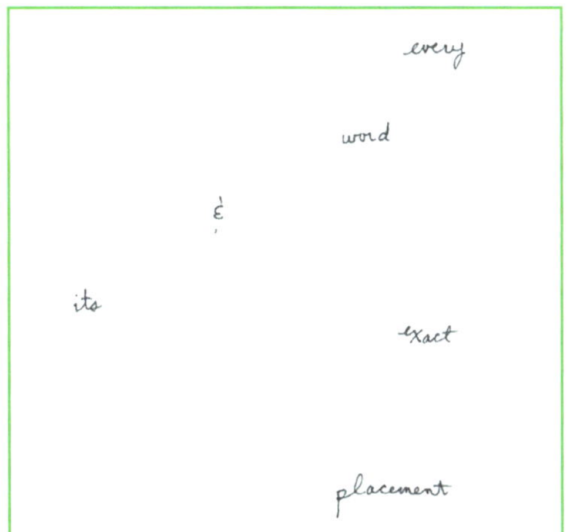

chax 2024

Cover art: Cal Wenby, *Edit*, mixed media & collage, 2022.
Thank you to the artist for permission to use this work.

ISBN 978-1-946104-57-1

Publisher's Cataloging-in-Publication Data

Names: Lazer, Hank.
Title: Abundant life : new & selected poems / Hank Lazer.
Other titles: Abundant life : new and selected poems.
Description: Tucson, AZ : Chax Press, 2025. | Summary: Includes poems selected from Lazer's fifteen poetry books published in the 21st century, along with a selection of new poems. Notes provide information about each of the previous books, and many kinds of poetries, including visual poetry, are included.
Identifiers: LCCN 2025932754 | ISBN 9781946104571 (pbk.)
Subjects: LCSH: American poetry – 21st century. | Zen Buddhism – Poetry. | Jews – Social life and customs – Poetry. | China – Poetry. | Cuba – Poetry. | LCGFT: Poetry. | Visual poetry. | BISAC: POETRY / American / General. | POETRY / Subjects & Themes / Religious. | POETRY / Subjects & Themes / Diversity & Multicultural.
Classification: LCC PS326.L39.A28 2025 | DDC 811--dc23
LC record available at https://lccn.loc.gov/2025932754

Chax Press
6181 E 4th St
Tucson Arizona 85711-1613
USA

Chax Press is a nonprofit 501(c)3 arts organization. Chax Press books are supported in part by individual donors and by sales of the books. Please visit *https://chax.org/membership-support/* if you would like to contribute to our mission to make an impact on literature and culture in our time.

In the past two years Chax has received grant support from the Arizona Commission on the Arts, the Arts Foundation for Tucson and Southern Arizona, and The Poetry Foundation. We thank our supporters, without which our work would not be possible.

With thanks

to David Antin, Robert Creeley, Larry Eigner, & Lyn Hejinian

still alive, read, & listened to

Contents

From *Days* (2002)

3

10/1/94

and then again back
in it witness
serendipitous atoms drip
& cripple the im
perceptible ache of it
jack she *took* her
life a parent's love
called a darkening
of the heart emily to
susan avalanche or avenue

5

10/4/94

quick zig zag attack
blue black ink jet
on stock white bond
thelonious all alone
hit hard the off beat
white space dark rec
tangular pitch arm or
tar which chuck called it
a clip joint chili davis
legged out the grounder

6

10/10/94

for they will differ if
they do as syllable
from sound this is
hers our round did she
shiver did she know
exactly the persistent
strangeness she had
written did she ultimate
circumference wheel no
hub

13

10/25/94

so masculine to cackle
go dumb born book
granite blocks glottal stops
& then went eddying forth
in ways one had done
previously   vatic beauty
well after spiritual
was ever tenable   effloresce
& clot back   the caption
or the azure elsewhere

14

11/7/94

either i'm as
far away from the
sacred as i've
ever been or it's
popping up here all
the time in
words   parquet   parole
part of the
overall or
not

15

11/13/94

he spoke
melodic idiom
bumfuzzled &
such stump
recrudescent vista
wipers flapping
syrupy flourish
grooved twosome
sack lunch
whose business

56

2/23/95

why miles
stuck the *about*
between *round* and
midnight i
nor monk'll
ever know
blow john blow
gauze gossamer
ghostly go
blow john blow

59

2/24/95

the entire curric
ulum bends mall
eable pixel flits rains
on parched defended square
acres augurs a renewed
dance of the intellect
paideuma of moving word icon
death dog rising over
nostalgic casual ashes muse
um of intensive reading

coolidge
registers p. 1

71

3/3/95

good god bob
you're the one
of course who
made loveable &
why the fuck
not in such
a tight span
these twists of
thinking specific
to an instant

72

3/4/95

we addicts of
intensity we see
& the angel
she has
the actual mouth
piece of the trumpet
in her mouth
& we hear blast
by blast until
we are broken down

howard finster

74

3/11/95

i sing the body
eclectic uh defective
icing the bawdy
directive rodin to young
rilke *"toujours travailler"*
all words & no fray
makes yack a dull
"stable & precarious"
rose on licorice er
icarus' wings

76

3/31/95 listen or voluptuous every after Mac Low
lord image great house thunder
your exact science
less ontology vicarious errand
linguistic instants grace heavenly tense
you've error skin
lunch on visionary errata
lovely ink grimace hidden turnabout
yellow elemental silence
liking impinges ghostly host thereafter

84

4/15/95

slow to slogan
voracious to
veracity amen
to mendacity
flesh to pleasure
legs to legendary
costly to apostle
mesh to measure
& i wake up
next to you

99

5/11/95 their drive then
too fragile or
drive he said &
why not as my great
uncle leon high
ball in hand said
his generation had
drive but mine
stoned was
pissing it away

138

7/3/95 fabric echoes fabri
cation you're making
that up &
country boy eddie
says   i never et
y mology i didn't
like   the local
not dirt but
deep down in the
vowels of the earth

205

9/13/95 yes that it
resists being
used up in taggart /207/ lecp
action re
turned to a
thousand times
ok maybe a
little less
nevertheless re
news re pays engagement

From *Elegies & Vacations* (2004)

For John Cage

we don't go
to find you there

you made it
and you are not there

in its making
you
were not its destination

as the canceled space
in your exact nature

you are there

§

you are there

in your exact nature
as the canceled space

were not its destination
you
in its making

and you are not there
you made it

to find you there
we don't go

Deathwatch for My Father

Charles Lazer September 29, 1926 – February 16, 1996

ever as in
light

12/2/95

one among the many
questions   why am i
writing   in the face of
your dying   (an event
by the way   that has
no face)   one among
your many doctors
says   with regret
yes   it is a matter
of days maybe at most
a few weeks
my mind inclines
to ask   and what
is *it* perhaps to
turn your death into
linguistic inquiry
a somewhat familiar
terrain   you say
from your hospital bed
"henry   the one thing i
regret about this disease
is that i have it instead
of moamar khadafy"
we *do* mostly at my
urging   cry together
and say out loud
our love for one another
but mostly your preference
(which i expect as i
get much older
will prove exemplary
though contrary to my
nature) is to talk
lightly   football games
the intricacies of golf

which you still hope
to play
i went
out this afternoon & played
a few holes hit some
practice shots walked alone
knowing the golf course
is one place i can always
contact you   this day
quite literally wearing one
of your shirts one of your
sweaters playing with
the blade irons you
bought from ben crenshaw
and gave to me
good thing i was alone
because my crying
(to someone else)
would have made no
sense   i began to think
about the last round
we played together
Cypress Point in june
amazingly a crystal clear
warm morning a dream
round at one of the world's
most beautiful courses
a reprieve from your
leukemia   a gift from
a friend   a day to be
savored your way
immersed in our
mostly silent companionship
for the course itself
gave us enough to
think about

as a poet
to think about
that last round
takes me to a rhetorical
hazard   the emotional msg
the flavor enhancing phrases

of the manipulative personal
poem   the vast litany
of "for the last time,"
"finally," "never again,"
"suddenly" "even"
"so much" "ultimately"
"if ever" etcetera
in golf these phrases
amount to hitting the shot
fat   you have been
a major part of my poems
since i wrote "point sur"
in 1972 though clearly
poems are not much like
you   in fact i imagined
yesterday telling a friend
"we can only love
purely and fully
someone quite different
from ourselves"
and i had you in
mind   though i know
the generalization like
most to be untrue

in my poetry class
i am teaching george oppen
a poet of the greatest
integrity one still interested
in truth   he would i know
encourage me (& perhaps has
in writing this poem) to
test poetry in the face
of the worst events

if the words have value
they have value there too

so we come to a place
of dwindling conversation
of friends calling and crying
with you   of walkers
and wheelchairs and
hospice   of your softening

voice your constricted
throat
            a long putt
dying at the hole
the ball does turn &
drop but believe me
it's no occasion for joy
we've played
we play
it's a shot
we've got to hit

loss installs itself
among us beckons

ever lapsing light

12/6/95

here we are
together again
as desired
let us say yes
to where we
find ourselves
& to what
must happen
let us say
yes to the time
we do have
as it is given
to us to dwell
there equably
& i will witness
with you going
as i can
knowing this
as privilege
awe &
awful
the opening you
are entering

not one prinCipally given to words
but works Hard these
lAst days
to wRite a series of thank you notes
the one to warren worries him a Lot
hE can't get it right
with the noSe

bLeeds the
trAnsfusions and the other interruptions
not exactly a craZy last task but an
odd choicE
for he has been typically a moRe quiet though heartfelt correspondent

§

this is his wrong though givEn name the way
fanya Spelled it
legally hiS
but never what i heArd him called

§

he seleCted
cHarles after his father's "chaim"
and then as he told it with a shrUg
the guys Called him
chucK

§

grace & concentration in
athletics exactness no
bullshitting & he wouldn't
taught & expected
practice & rapt
attention that
there is
the prospect of
getting it right

which he
on occasion
did

hard to believe
for example
at Pasatiempo
(both witnessed)
a week apart
on the same hole
made double eagle

& at the end of his life
submitted gladly to
by his standards playing
badly the game the playing
the companionship the beauty
of the place superior
to individual accomplishment

by my uncle stan's conjecture chuck woulD rather go off
awaY from us not be a bother an
off rhyme wIth the
Native american custom the old one ill
wanderinG off to die alone

does he know he won't make it to hawaii
or does he express the wish to go there for our
benefit to give us and him some hope for his strength
some modest reprieve an unexpected few extra
days he says he would go knowing he would not
come back   he says there he could count on
being warm   being in the sun   is this
the simple boy from san jose taking with his wife
one last glorious vacation   or some unconscious
desire to be like the hawaiians   a ceremony
he has seen   the outrigger canoes paddling
away from diamond head   orchid petals
scattered on the sea   and finally his ashes
scattered too   these questions are *my*
conjectures   he has expressed his wishes simply
with no intention   i suppose   of being enigmatic

12/8/95

against death upon
mom's desk i see
the several
books: *perfect*
health & *love,*
medicine, & miracles
today i will
price out rates
for cremation
in the grim
humor we share
you say
"son, get me
a good deal"

and i will
since the acute
& confusing grief
is for now
a way's away

when you told me you wanted cremation you told me about your conversation with dr. pearlstein as he neared death. he too chose cremation, but he so hated the predatory mortuary business that he researched california law, the pertinent specification: "must be cremated in a suitable container." those last two words gave the funeral homes their opening -- "wouldn't you want your loved one etc." dr. pearlstein specified in his will that he wished to be cremated, and that in keeping with california law, he wished to be cremated in "a suitable container." which he specified as a large brown paper bag.

12/11/95 – return – airplane

crying has tired my eyes

being distant above the earth is fine

being high up & going against the erasing clouds is fine

the anger at the arrangements that didn't work out

can be seen now as a desirable acting out
specifically which items will be given away
can be taken care of later

organ donation probably won't work out
since he has a blood disease

they might take his eyes

simple cremation will be easier to arrange
than expected donna at the mortuary
did not try to sell me lots of extras
we can use our own urn
we can scatter the ashes
whenever we wish
a simple fibreboard box
may house the body
the cremation will be done locally
there will be no mileage charge
for pick up

it is best to gather the obituary information
ahead of time
there are many papers to fill out
there are various benefits to consider
veterans social security and the like

he said definitely "no formal service
& none of that rabbi crap"

people could come back
to the house to eat & talk
that would be ok

lucidity humor no acute pain
a strange way to be dying

§

though we may think so
we are not special
unique yes but not special

§

it is just
dying

& it requires
great cooperation

amidst the crying
you learn
a certain singing

§

the flowering of a particular
tenderness in his voice
calling out “henry”
and then as i sit
on the bed beside him
that new voice
asking about donating his organs
or giving his saws and miter box
to someone who might need them
a gentle assertive voice
expressive
quite peaceful
really

12/22/95

ever exacting
light

it cannot be told
not his life not
the dying not a single
day cannot be
told properly cannot be
told fully not
possible to account for

the fine gradations
of change the in
explicable shiftings
from weaker to stronger
& back again not
possible to be exactly
faithful to any
instance the nose
begins to bleed &
then it stops
zeno's arrow is
always in trans
it & every breath
is the same as
a last breath
which we who
love him listen
for and listen
toward trying to
distinguish one
from another when
a true telling
would enter into
the precisely in
distinct the anon
ymously individual
gray gradations
of the arrow's
consequential
but unknowable
flight
we talk instead
of smoked salmon
a dill potato bread
jane found at
vincent's a roasted
new potato salad
the hungers
of an instant

choy ling calls
unaware of how
sick you are

not knowing you
cannot go to hawaii
that you won't make
her new year's party
she among the living
& crying with you on the phone
through the sobbing you do
tell her to give to charity
all you have stored over there

mom yesterday was certain
you were dying certain
it would be soon
too weak to sit up
too weak to turn over in bed
two hours later
you called me
feeling better
and we talked about
food and football
moving as we all seem to
from certainty to certainty
none encompassing
all that much
never quite on the mark

§

knowing this   to partial

to be   departures

the arrow   going

of my ways   going slowly

partial by   degrees

§

12/27/95

judicious
use

his vanishing
voice

says only
i

am very
tired

§

the i itself is tired out, gives way to the generic human, foetal, painfully dependent, unable to move on its own, the steady weight loss, distended belly, teeth no longer fit right scrape and bruise the gums, food loses its appeal, the voice grows softer, a pitiful whisper, still articulate, still lucid, amidst the terrible embarrassment of every act requiring help, how else to sit up, or shave, or urinate, how else to bathe, or eat, or shit, inside the battle between acceptance and anger, resignation and self-pity, as ever his specific behavior (the i that does survive) placid, equable, humorous, nonetheless in the context of more encompassing sleep

suffused
in light

12/29/95

once again an
experimental
drug: *leukine*
just approved
& you begin the
shots   that

& another drug
for your mouth
some way to
break the pain
to change the
starvation diet
gums too sore
to slobber through
matzo ball soup
flown up from LA

sammy your nurse
suspects the gum
sores may be a
sign of thrush

an odd name
when you think
about it for a
disease of mouth
& throat a
fairly common fungus
in infants

did Frost
in his
pastoral exactness
have this in
mind when he
wrote "thrush
music – hark!"
a harking up
a constricted
music strangling
the rush
the babe placed
among the bul-
rushes floats toward
or sticks in the
throat of
some dumb destiny

"Far in the pillared dark
Thrush music went –

Almost like a call to come in
To the dark and lament"
Frost answered back
"I would not come in"
& gave his numerous
specific refusals
so much was he
secretly in love
with grief
and the vigor
of his own resistance

and you have said
equally clearly
you will come in:

if these two
medicines do not
work you have
told dr. rubin
to leave you alone

this
i understand

§

1/3/96

and for a time
the new drugs
seem to work

one morning
the sores
all of them
fall out of
your mouth

& you begin to
walk again

you go out
you visit
mom sells the
business

the mystical *chi*
for a time is restored
i savor each
phone call
the daily confirmation
of your renewed
voice your will
under these conditions
to live

oddly
at the hospital
the blood numbers
red white platelet
show no
significant change

§

1/5/96

is the poem co
incident with
your own stepping
over
                what
reasonably of the two
can be fused

if you as yesterday
get to the restaurant
& find you cannot
get out of the car
& that mom must
therefore take you home

under such conditions
what is it that the poem
is obligated to do
professions of love
seem perfunctory
though i know too
the best elegies
are early & often

when the love has been
clearly if not inventively
stated   the poem
then does what it
always does
among other things
mark time

§

1/6/96

of sudden
of a sudden

of books
the sudden love
so these
could be the one
tee-tum

a dumb surprise
among
the panoply of singings

your rhythm
dad
of absolute
interest
day to day
hour to hour

if i call you
every day
if i call you
every hour
i can get down to
an increment of time
in which change
cannot take place

that anti
epiphanic space
the im
perceptible
modulation
of current circumstance

not repetition
but as stein
had it
minute
differences in
insistence

and somehow
everyone comes to be
an old one

and when we
look closely
very closely

"it is a very
difficult thing
to know anything
of the being
in any one"

§

1/9/96

terri said maybe you *are*

after all in this reprieve
getting to have
some of an "old age"
crotchety   focused
talking about this
sonofabitch
& telling the handyman
who's late again
and unprepared
he's full of shit
worried too about
your teeth their fit
their slippage on your gums
and goddamned if anyone's
going to pester you into
eating when you've decided
you won't   hurray i say
for all your asinine
stubbornness the vigor
of your resistance an
imperfect pain in the ass
a role til now
you had been forgetful of

§

a poem a cell
the structures of activity
motion coincident with
a complex equation
as you move

through space & time

§

a
precise nature
of dying
is that it doesn't
seem

to be going
on
and
because that *is*
the case
we honestly
don't much
turn our attention
to
it

§

words
the similar
ciphers

the poem
determined
by the length
of your life

i don't know
for you
whether it's comforting
or upsetting
to know there are
memorials such as this
being built for you

a pyre
a crypt
similar ciphers

pixel
of light
released
beneath the letters

§

1/12/96

as had been proud
not the least of which
the supple single words
i have in this intended
& asking of you as you
the exact metric   made of blanks

you'd love to see   (& i would too)
the Packers kick the shit out of the Cowboys

"except walking expressly"   *cell* / *lyn hejinian* / 20

saxophone
his blowing adequate to being
blew it no simpler than it is
exactly scratchy   her voice
very melodic

so obviously not

consecutive
accumulating
somehow nonetheless

§

1/13/96

so long as i am
reading this particular
book   of final
conversations with
john cage   you will
                        no need to
complete the equation

in this the miraculous

the stretched temporary
of adequate duration
lose gratitude
return to more normative
structures of diffuse
attention
you not central to every
thought you not the boss
of tragic narrative

words again go out to play
sniff other shrubs
seep morph shift stutter
heuristic twist
“thought’s torsion”
in the instant
of its thinking

healthy
or moreso
as each
injected with
the experimental
which in this
instance
opens up
time
& some of it
together

leukemia
to lupine
the beautiful
pea pod

§

1/14/96

rough
as a cob

difficult

as herding cats

so as you go
you are changing
your thinking in
relation to it

told me in detail about garzone's
bad investment   not everyone wants
a contemporary look & at 895
who wants to share a drive
way   & radiant heat scares
people

we don't know
if our own experiences
are especially typical
i enjoy your company
and our conversations

i have no idea
whether it's that way
for most sons
i hope with my own
son we will talk
to each other with
mutual interest well
into my old age
work to imagine

§

1/18/96

speaking
relatively
a spell
of approximate
health
& utterly
improbable

§

1/27/96

& so pre
sent a present
of

trips to costco
orchard supply
trader joe's
an evening conducting
the annual homeowners'
meeting   each day
some major outing
a lunch   a trip
to the office
then you stood up
took a shower
shampooed your hair
dressed yourself
barely needing the walker

you've driven the new
car once or twice
went then at mom's
insistence to show
your doctor what was
happening
shocked him
into a thorough exam
the white count doubled
the platelets doubled
no one talks of
recovery or exactly
what this miracle
is or isn't
a reprieve an
unexpected return
of strength

as with most
other living
unforeseen

1/28/96

for carrying
or calibrating
test results yield
specific momentary data

vs. your
subjective impression

the two generally
in parallel

extremely precise &
thus precisely enigmatic

telling jokes again
slowly   & drawn out
“henry   there were these three doctors
who died & went before St. Peter
to find out if they would get into heaven
the first doctor said, ‘i devoted my life to cancer research;
i made some small discoveries   i tried my best.’
st. peter said, ‘ok you get to go to heaven’
the second doctor said, ‘all my life i served the poor
i never made much money   i saved the ones i could’
st. peter said, ‘ok   you get to go to heaven’
the third doctor said, ‘i developed four of the largest
HMOs in the region’   st. peter thought
then said, ‘for you i’ve got some good news
& some bad news   the good news is you get to go to heaven
the bad new is   you can only stay three days’”

a return to banality
nothing particularly evil there

no intensifying difference
back to the oblique   the deflected *a re*
turn or retreat into ungraspable dailiness

1/31/96

consecutively
the succession
of his thoughts
become projects
some of which
he must get
done stubborn
is another way
to put it
& like his mother
what he's stubborn
about
will not
get talked out
the garage his clothes the files
a set of metonyms
at what duration
does time become
significant
cherished in short
spans
at some length & beyond
inevitably banal

he does much more
thinking
i know it

2/3/96

i have the luxury of waiting
& you have the refusal to eat most foods
& mom may begin to sell the place in honolulu
& slowly you are
cleaning & rearranging the garage

moving as we do
unnoticed
through our variable temporal relations
yours   (& thus ours, in part)
from cherish to grateful
to the more familiar tub
of routine daily bathing
from time felt & pondered
now returned
in what we call
reprieve or
miracle
restored to the illusion
of endlessness
the merciful indistinctness
of its
(actually our)
disappearance

rather than your
daily worsening
the markers become again
sporting events & the weather
Magic's return
as a power forward
Phil Mickelson's seven straight one-putts
to win the tournament
your sunshine & our winter storm

here sporadic snow flakes
a few birds rummage
among the sharp holly bushes
the iced over roads
(blank paper-like
with a few semi-
visible habitual tracks)
stop us

2/16/96
Dallas to San Jose

of love

the decisive one

again flying west
this time with some
finality
after his extended reprieve
a disappearance of
the expressively heroic
the miraculous last
burst of doing
the atypical heart
felt conversations

these last two weeks
principally foetal
the generic sleeping
little ability or desire
to eat or drink

then peeing the bed
a bad fall &
his body pinned
between the wall
& the toilet

a day in the hospital
more transfusions
but no change
in energy level
conversation
a whisper in which
he claims to be
in no pain claims
to be comfortable

dr. rubin
determines you
won't leave the hospital
that the leukemic cells
have taken over

anyone's touch

is painful to you

you have promised
to hang on
until i arrive
these narrative
arrangements
are not ours
to make

if you die
before i arrive
that is fine
especially if it
is a good
& easy death

as for my wishes
i would gladly
sit with you
the sporadic whispered
conversations a
holding of your hand
the unfocused
opening of your eyes

love calls us
or so i feel
to the whole cycle
of a loved one's
life the dying too
is holy that time
together sacramental
instructive
intimate
enigmatic

when i spoke with you
yesterday on the phone
your humor remained
intact   after a long
pause   you asked
still mocking your

mother & the recurrent
question of her
senility in her 95th year
"so how's bigshot?"
and i told you
what alan, now
seven, was doing
that afternoon

i didn't tell you
that he prayed
for you & that he
asks with tenderness
and abstract curiosity
about what the leukemia
is   and what it's
doing to you

oddly
on the way to his
school two
days ago we
heard radio news
of a promising
canadian treatment
for leukemia

§

for many years
i have been
blessed & protected
by the outposts
of four grandparents
they are gone now
and you will die
& i
will cease to be
a son

more mornings
come

a few times
every day

of
the dying
the living
die
into

it matters:
your night nurse
is jewish
she's been she says
much among
the dying
& you she says
are not quite
there yet
& will make it
til i get there
& maybe
a day or so
beyond

as then
the final man

we age into
a caricature
of our pre
decessors

2/29/96

to yearn
in the dirction
one is

to do so
fully

without reservation

he
seemed to
do so
&
died
having moved
to an interior

for a time
he had
the capacity
to whisper

to raise
his right hand
sometimes to grasp
one of ours

sometimes to lay it

on his own chest
& moan

closed eyes
shallow breathing

a shot
of morphine

an hour
or so
later

the eyes
rolled back

& that
was
that

call it
peace
or
an end

from
which
a million
narratives
depart
a flow
of emotion

as best i
know by
the term
kensho

that kind of
flash
which
changes a life
(mine i
know)

thereafter
each new
instance
of human
consolation

simultaneously
heals
&
tears open

§

Wendy had given you permission to quit struggling,
to "go be with god." Odd, I thought, she's never once
I can recollect ever said anything about god.
Earlier, she
had thrown herself on you sobbing, "he never did anything
mean to anyone in his life." I said, "oh yes he did. The first
golf club he gave me, when I was five, was a one iron." And you,
already losing speech, had not, two hours from death, lost your

sense of humor, and you chuckled and gave a faint smile.
You
rallied
just enough to acknowledge mom's presence, my presence, Terri's,
and Stan and Linda's. But you were fully into yourself, or
somewhere
else.   You are gone. We go on.

3/6/96

there is a

O
R C
K

in the stream
around which
the water flows

§

if not
the physical body
what are we

From *The New Spirit* (2005)

3

you could tune it   some other way   apparent to
rhythmic conviction   insistent   as you have it   as it
manifests itself   filtered breeze   crisp circle   these sudden elements
sent as breath   said silently   or as actually spoken

what can be heard
what can be now attended
to   *hear this*
the exact metaphysics
of your historical

moment of listening
what does not change   is the
will or   disposition to listen
what does change   is
which rhythms   which combinations of sounds   what music one
in his or her time   is inclined   to listen
to
perhaps *close* listening   but more exactly   *beckoned* listening
audition
summoned from the criss-cross   of your historical circumstance

*

too logopoeia please   stop sermon   cross cut bright elements

fiery filaments shine   *vishnu leeshma corazón*   bright strive honk

talk tongues unclench   to eloquent extension   a pirouette a

parachute for you   a piece of parchment   an arrowhead

a tool for   breaking up compelled incorporation   to speak

of something else   enabled by shaping   breath to turn

Invocation

sum up what you know   you know enough by
now   sing out   what til now   you've kept to yourself
& so declare the daring done

                                                  so said the voice   the cadence
in which i heard it
                                   breath & ink   fibers so entwined

*

silver   that color   please   i ask you   please   (what place?)

                                                                                          *

short order   short circuit   shirk it   the shirt you designed the one
your grandmother fanya sewed   on her old treadle machine   an 1880s Singer
that shirt has a priest's collar   why now do you wish to avoid public profession
even as you seek it

                              *

                                        his death   a final step
panting as a dog

*

your guess as to what   becomes usable

the memorable   not subject to prior manipulation   that scene
his labored breathing   continues to obliterate all others   father

i ask   where are you

*

harsh quarrel   raised voice
of intimate anger   complaint & disappointment   love   love   inextricable

no end to knowing   you know you know   by casting off &
adding on   & every few years or more   some sudden clarification
sinks in   & disappears
pleasures of an abiding calm
riding odd cadences of knowing

*

and staring up to stare   face tilted into autumn light   an attitude
of thinking   a surface   upon which to imagine

*

who else   but your young son one day at his sketch pad   to draw
the gateway between being and non-being   human shapes   emerging
& receding

each   lives within a different hearing   given to each
that babel   attunes   our differential   thinking / singing   choral
gathering of each genetic specificity

difference difference difference

the common

denominator

in the name of specific rhythmic

in the name of *is*

yakov awoke   changed by the knowing

slipped messages into
oblique code of words   insistence   who's there   it   is

*

who that man

transmission interrupted

*

if given a life   in the study of words

had been a visitant
had listened   had heard whispers

wind   & intricate perfect

movement   body of leaves   that ornamental pear tree across the street
these fall days   preceding golden

connecting next to next

to

*

one other who has no job who has some money learns
he is an anchor a light warrior altering & saving the place where
he lives receives words & explanations from another who writes down what he
is told from ones on the other side

to say so in certain ways

gets crazy

no known plate tectonics for the invisible

i hear it i hear you this is the medium here
we are say it for yourself

*

call it crocks

of regional shit trendy mysticism of the under-employed & so
get busy

and what if

amid crocks of digital

cacophony

and what if

*

and shed the day

in sleep   arise afresh   in gratitude   in dawn light

“the pulsing life of sound”

6

in this world whose ear suzy o when the

saints i want to be there *"plumb crazy core"*

road side desert to desire wander in that number

yes money money first you can tell that's what
young want & see us as quaint or liars
if we say otherwise
gone down mid sudden mysteries

*

soul upon waters soul in air soul goes thinking

scribe sky soonest mended shut eyes embrace shining after-image

verb without complication
that state of being
air bubbles
rise to surface & burst as we are lived

bells toll

each quarter-hour arrives   departs

reaches the surface

against that face

bursts   bell-toll absorbed   within recurring sky

*

go there   gather as you hear   given circuits in

many languages urge   prayer whisper petition   rise into light

forever ever moved   dance by daily steps to an

altar   in that number   seven times seven years   arrive

at daily gratitude   wake into light   be there [   ]

in that number   love that morning   soul upon waters

teshuvah: heading south

this or that   or some such thing   chuck when talking
about a person's capabilities   called it *wherewithall*   toward the
middle   trane played just ahead of any sense he already understood

*

bless departed ronald johnson who wrote

anemone mnemonic
to the least   *ARK* 43
loomed am

but for absolute bond density   none better   than zukofsky
though ronald could sure as hell slow you down:

at taps   *ARK* 41
aft twilit lilac panicle

rafter   beam   arch   colonnade

a cupola fran & ollie show   what's all the hoopla?

chant a rant against the useful dance   thinking of

living   of most instances of a few minutes   honestly

you'd have to say *"what plot?"*

*

when the saints   came final things

or better yet   to very best

could be consideration will be given

could be we won't wait in line   after all *they* are marching in

could be the doors   could be the hallway   could be the governor will
unfold his arms & step aside

*

if *flowers say it best*   what exactly is it   that flowers say?

lord always then of being
homecoming starts with laughs

*

star

spire   fly forth into   seven elements

fled then into unraveled latitudes   loose   to lucid

cupboard   of summer syllables   foment a cooling firmament

bright hooves break along

*

furnished according to

*

reveals his glory   early in the morning

*

we are much older   than this would suggest

so it might

here   become itself   & here (& there)   of adequate complexity

singing as the sign   singing as *dasein*   assign the singing to

our being here & there

*

my uncle tells me that neurophysiology
research now shows that in order to see   the eye must move constantly   must
make tiny movements   so that the receptors are not over-saturated by
a single image

*

we came across frozen archipelagoes

*

crossed wolf river   ran along a road of words

listened in the forward movement   of john's blue train

distance is time & miles minutes   crossed hobolochitto creek

linguistic visitant   beloved decadent protectorate   & crossed it again

& then the pearl river

*

tend the flowers   change by season   john the stuttered

phrase accumulated   layered phrasing piling   on the seed

words **rose memory** **problem chapel crying** **vibration** *"led on*
by music" "in the middle of my life" necessity

*

finite times to return to this room that measures years

to this room home of light loom permitted to return

finite as in count your blessings
for each one count
this one

having found that compact concatenation
percussive sister

*

a constrained white boy's chant

but damn john
it swings anyway

soul swings to its own dissatisfactions
that the soul's genetic map hitched rhythm

that & a whole lot more

(the risk of course being flatness)

*

even with as much as gets forgotten
what is   is unforgettable

much worth knowing   or trying to know
be sure to know

or try to   what love is   & where it exists   as a force
apart from specific persons

better yet
whatever it is
have it sing

words on the page   its bodily choreography

the children get older
which means your own function

grows increasingly retrospective
or prospective   & insistent in ways that for others
your vision has no context

you chose a set of odd nutrients

& now you're precisely where they've

gotten you

when the saints

in *that* number

*

no specific door

or the best words of others

these readings then *teshuvah* no other pur

pose but the turning

7 x 7 years

the first time through

all seven cycles then begin again

with gratitude

& growing stress

on retrospect

speak it & sing it

when these had been forbidden

speak it & sing it

resources

begin again

when the senses

as before

the seed phrase must be adequate

to words in permutations

that death not expected

*

crossed wolf river ran along a road of words

listened in the forward movement of john's blue train

distance is time & miles minutes crossed hobolochitto creek

linguistic visitant beloved decadent protectorate & crossed it again

& then the pearl river

8

(in transit)

three little words   *teshuvah* turn toward   you no more

dramatic than this   car moving in   & out of

shadows i love   you & i   have chosen wrong

live with it   three little words   when the saints

when something great   bags & trane   in that number

turn & turn   felt a sharp   turn at 49

*

son at sea lab   cut the squid open   found
the ink sac

slowly we learn   to work alone
&   with each other

three little words

baruch atah

adonai

love what is

& where you are

take

dictation

or quit altogether

user pays connection fee

drove

south thinking about this or that lush southern sound

*

gateway   i'm here   *shma yisroel adonai*   three word suite

hear o israel   versus nervous be-bop   soul attentive to

its own amusements   play it loud   lord our god

through whatever horn   breathe & shape   heavenly blue legacy

golden fall light   drove me down   the river delta

ghostly sax   tilted back   succession then   when the saints

From *Portions* (2009)

Falls
—Yosemite

vernal falls crashes
down with steady
force from feeding

stream down to
river winding through
boulders canyoned channeled

flow   this is
pure manifestation of
shekinah such is

this force that
flows & upholds
that makes possible

every instant &
everything that is
in being   we

move on the
current of mercy
the river merced

Turning

coffee   dawn   light
eyes turn into
the word wake

slowly awake to
deliberate a word
at a time

waves arrive wake
deliberately to determined
slow movements of

the writing hand
will not tell
at all until

eyes move slowly
along the chosen
words a rising

symphony of the
busy eyes turning
to this world

First

he is bruised
we hold them
dear as ornament

given over to
a music others
manage to ignore

he is bruised
loyal to an
invisible almost comic

dare we say
order compelled then
we may say

ordered light foot
strides first memorable
instance of magic

chanting bid bidding
to abide with
to be among

Dream

dream we then
of every step
the home our

body made of
interface as we
objectify ourselves bit

by bit reprogram
splice heal redirect
reconvene what we

are   texture of
tense repaired   dream
we then &

sing of our
new relations to
time milling ourselves

to new specifications
dream we then
of every step

Avant

avant   i want
& if you
i am becoming

my father's dying
body   okra   tomatoes
sweet corn   sunflower

to my son
our neighbor says
"you look just

like your father"
beans   field peas
new potatoes   today's

purchase   or to
gain purchase   terror
of bare relation

just now   being
here   it of
course slips away

Religion

the city didn't
exist   going to
the country meant

ten minutes &
cows   my father's
father drove along

a happy man
if so not
in a contemporary

american sense   he
with the given
name Chaim   &

his wife Fanya
drove slowly with
a slight smile

they sang folk
songs in russian
& in yiddish

*

the cows were
not far from
town   the big

city meant San
Francisco on a
slow highway with

lots of stoplights
this would be
a sunday afternoon

in hebrew i
am told there
is no word

that means “*religion*”
for how or
why extract that

experience that emotion
from the surroundings
of everything else

Sense

sense the living
god with palms
upturned or say

three or four
right words turn
return sense the

palms with living
god upturned right
words return three

four calypso apocalypse
dance along peninsula
look down fissures

sense the living
with upturned her
brother stayed behind

& they killed
him living god
with palms upturned

Questions

i think i
knew there were
always questions you

put us in
position to have
these questions as

our lives i
think the best
questions go away

& return with
different force with
implications a previously

unfamiliar familiarity i
cannot abide plurals
& here they

are why is
this what you
do with us

Figure (3 x 18 x 2 for LZ)

so the syllogism
from one sound
others to hear

clearly to tell
one from another
to tell that

one is like
another that the
torsion or the

tearing of the
gears that the
thinking or the

thinking singing that
the fugue is
a figure go

figure in the
poem to figure
it out caring

*

zero carry the
one a funny
way to say

ten in her
care in his
an ear a

music made manifest
vhen de rebbe
singt throw in

the kitchen sink
paul will play
it he can

hear it thoughts'
torsion as cousin
george saw it

miracle that there
is something anything
to stand upon

Torah

every day when
i arise i
carry the torah

bear it aloft
for the torch
that it is

carry it burning
& unconsumed into
the darkness of

the day unable
to find a
temple i keep

alive the memory
of the Temple
destroyed the torch

becomes the ash
the blossom of
my father's bones

Shem

again & again
sit at night
beside the dark

window a flash
of lightning close
by then steady

drizzle i have
been given to
sit beside off

to the side
hidden especially hidden
from others hidden

but fully aware
dazzling glint momentary
blade fact is

good name the
good name of
i think it

You

—for Robert Creeley

so the old
cabin leans "*sit*
up" i said

as if to
someone i said
it to you

i always do
if there were
no one else

if there were
only you i
would say "*sit*

up" & think
someone heard such
is my sense

the old cabin
leans what is
never passes away

Good

the good song
finally the good
song in mind

thinking the good
song thinking &
singing it through

the good the
song consequent keeping
it in mind

a vessel for
carrying it for
bearing or igniting

the good song
attuned to the
hum of being

steady hum of
fluorescence the body's
own good song

Adjust

for the eyes
to adjust &
the darkness become

visible past woods'
edge a shadow
moves the trees

are simply trees
with opaque intensity
knee high thin

blanket of fog
over the mowed
field a friend

carries with him
horrible vivid memory
of a similar

place another walks
here ecstatic it
being this simple

Father

father of darkness
father in darkness
father gone over

into darkness farther
& farther ten
years & where

are you if
not here a
winter storm birds

huddled around the
feeder *"how 'bout*
them apples" i

come to these
words they feed
us they are

your living body
winter star light
wind & darkness

Book

small book secret
book blessed are
the singers book

tucked in crook
of arm book
hidden in your

sleeve a few
choice words secret
names a phrase

or two momentum
of blessing a
question scorned are

the questioners rich
text hyper link
volcanic text you

fall into walking
along eyes straight
ahead saying it

House

pad pod site
preparing a place
a launching pad

a landing site
small birds chickadees
finches sparrows ride

out arctic wind
bobbing on suspended
bird houses hung

from pine branches
small words as
on an ever

moving sea we
live & breathe
riding upon this

language house a
moving place that
feeds & carries

From N18 *(Complete)* (2012)

the shape doesn't
matter half as much
as you think it would really it's
more like the way you go about seeing
the pleiades making out that cloudy
set by looking a bit to the side
shape being a way to keep looking to the side

8/12/10

every

word

&

its

exact

placement

8/16/10

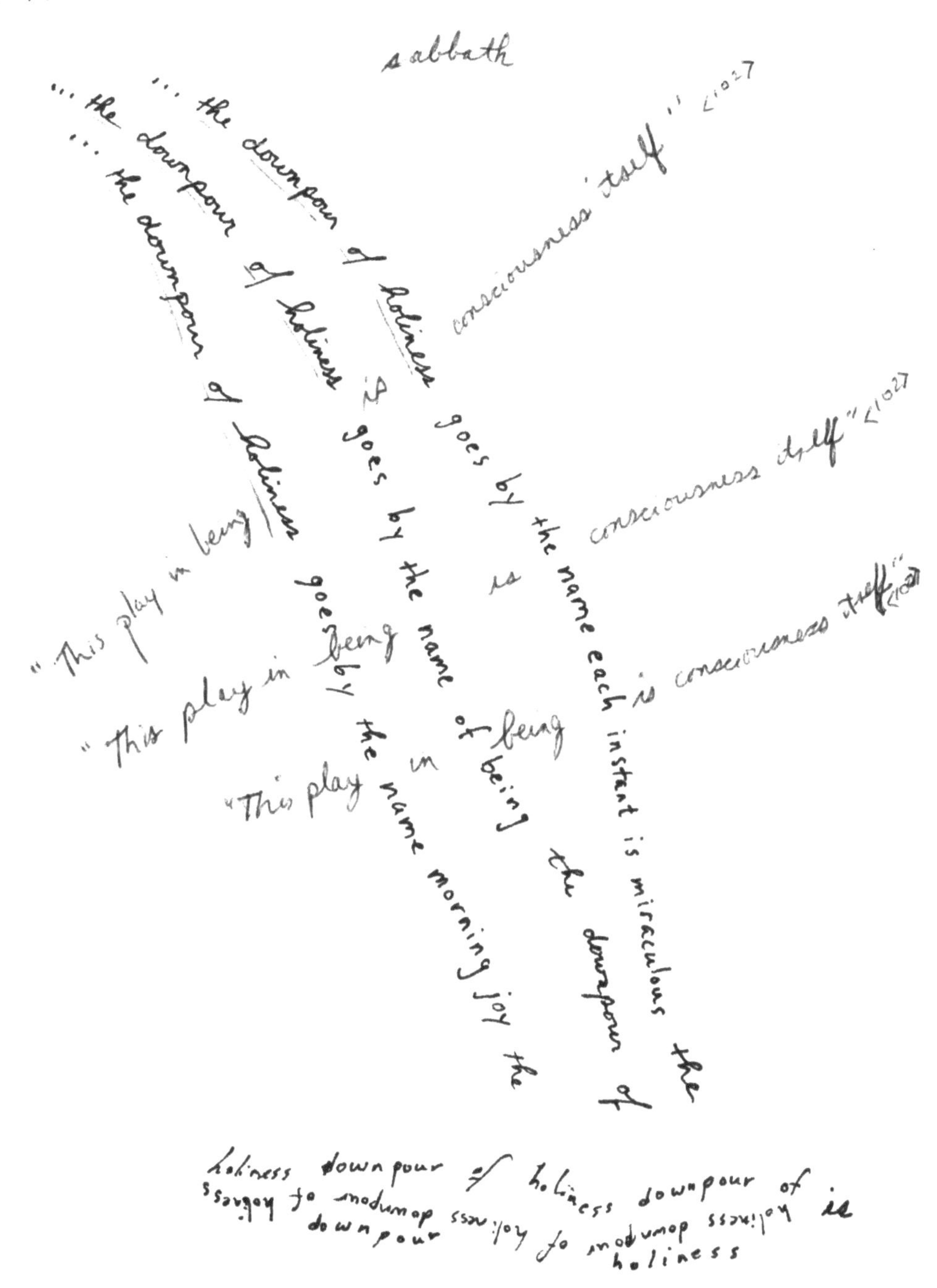

"on the nullification of oneself"
AS/57

a page

a day

keeps the doctor

(oy vay)

9/19/10
5771

THE BOOK A SPIRITUAL INSTRUMENT

page the door of the new year •

these two scientific visionaries the two Michaels from LA they told of an emerging human future as with the ongoing complex dance of the human brain & language we have entered into an irreversible merging with the high speed digitized virtual world of our making the human home having moved from nature to technology so that this physical world in its fragile varied beautiful exactitude may be left behind to other creatures while we begin to merge with the infinitely complex images of the rapid hybrid world where silicon & carbon life have fashioned a new consciousness an unforeseen second life the new home for what was human

10/2/10

you will find your own balance here

between

crossing

irony & faith

"It is to hold onto oneself while gnawing away at oneself." ⟨114⟩

"What is at stake for the self, in to being, is not to be." ⟨117⟩

& even when you choose faith

it will come & go

& the evidence for being

& your newly learned feeling for it

10/3/10

if you stare at the wall the same wall every morning - & practice your breathing you will come to see how interesting & varied the wall is in my case simple charcoal painted beige you will see the changing angles texture & intensity of the seasonal light the imperfections & shadowy tones of the wall itself perhaps

you will orient yourself by means of a slightly upraised dot barely visible which you might imagine to be the face of g-d or you may discover that if you stare at a spot intently it will disappear or you may learn that the wall itself is a guest & generative emptiness a doorway made solid by praying & silent waiting

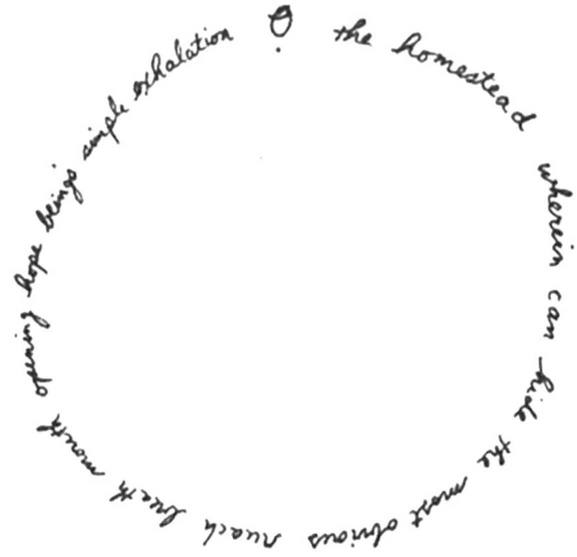
O the homestead wherein can hide the most obvious reach such mouth opening hope being's simple exhalation

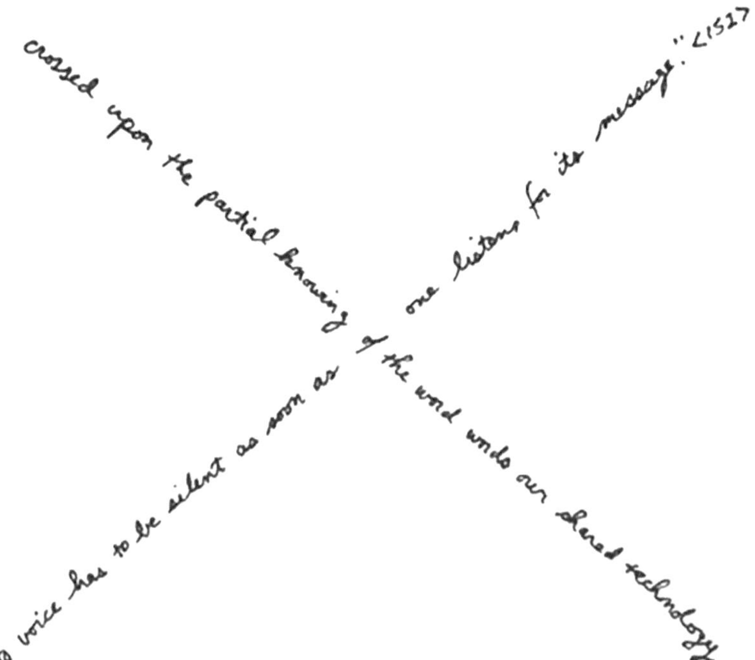
crossed upon the partial knowing of the word undo our shared technology
"Its voice has to be silent as soon as one listens for its message." <152>

12/11/10

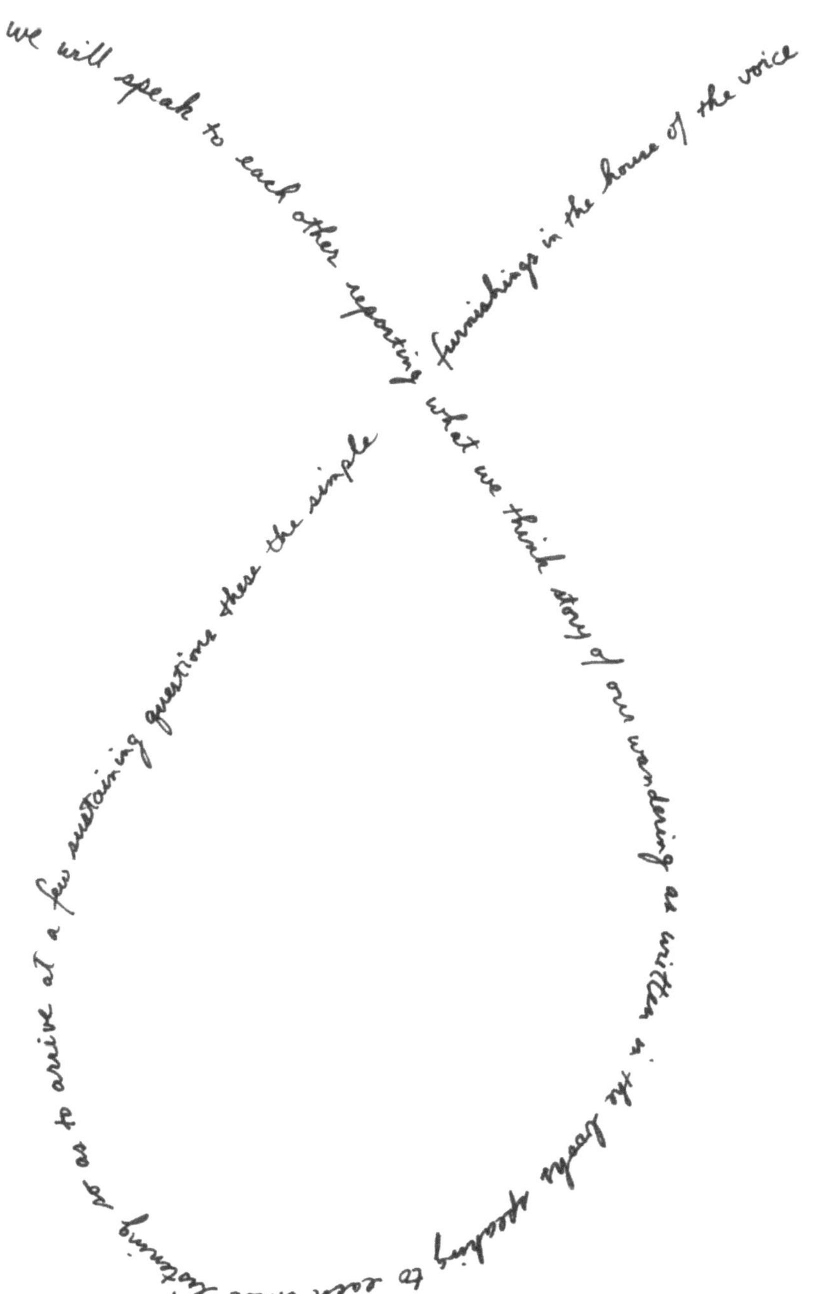
we will speak to each other reporting what we think story of our wandering as written is the books speaking to each other listening so as to arrive at a few sustaining questions these the simple furnishings in the house of the voice

if on a winter's day a reader if years from now or if suddenly now in a morning's clarifying light if prologue or prelude to whatever love might come your way if who we ; are turning the page together if verse itself is a version of turning ; returning together of hanging on through the tightest turns if on a winter's day if this day riding together we arrive if together we pause to take a reading may we hear as given guide as prelude that ever word onward

From *Poems Hidden in Plain View* (2016)

10/15/06

Kin as I am to an earthquake in Hawaii.

Coffee alters my relationship to time.   So too
the fall flowers   the last bloomings before the first
frost   before the leaves change color   before the grass
turns a dormant brown.   It is not though the seasons
that concerns me.   I want to know when are the seasons
felt as something personal & finite   as part of a limited
countdown   felt as a savored particularity.   Again,
the *fact* of being   the fact of time   not the object not
the what in time   but the medium itself   known through
its objects.

And where   most of the time   are brother &
sister   being & time   if not   behind you   or just out
of view   in the other room   or somewhere else waiting
for you to call.   They no doubt would have
their own questions to put to you.   They will.   They
will sketch them slowly upon your body until you
notice them.

And that invisibility is an essential
aspect of its ingenious construction.   So that we live
within it   *are* it   & only rarely feel it or reflect
upon it   or investigate it.

It will be slow going
writing reading thinking along through Heidegger's *Being & Time*
a book published the same year that Babe Ruth hit
60 homers.

There is a dead Virginia pine just beyond the back
fence.   My fourteen year old dog is going deaf.   My six year old
granddaughter is having an American Idol birthday party.   I like
them   but I have no faith in anecdotes.

I take it back.
I'm sure this preponderance of an abstract seemingly pointless

set of speculations becomes its own reductive mimesis
aping an invisible & amorphous time
                                                            Lyn's *Comedy* showed me
a way to have no form.   And so I took off.

                                                               Narrative presents
one small element of time's story.

                                                     Let's face it;   most of it
does not become a story.   End of subject.

                                                            An earth
quake   a snow storm   a gorgeous fall day   a memorial
symposium for the wondrous   Robert Creeley
                                                              now there's somebody
who felt time's variable metric   & mastered its lineation
or at least the primary stutter steps   the hesi
tations   & a kind of thinking happening staccato
like a bebop sax solo

12/16/06

to feel

& to attend to

intervals of consciousness

measured by

breath

1/7/07

we pray to pray
to be able to

to have that inclination
knowing that word *to*

brings with it a
host of uncertainties   constraints

& trivializing destinations   pray
as in engagement or

transmission crows in the
pines this dark morning

all that glitters *is*
try out what comes

to tongue think it
later already tuned to

the given music foot
steps a heart beat

gauging the weight &
mood   to count

on fact of black
mat succession of breaths

we pray to pray
to be able to

2/3/07

you
mean like
this when reading
gets turned on its side
you may think of the funnel & assert
that such thinking is now & that in these words
it then has a way of inching toward some bridge across
that unknowable station called the present with
its gift for a bewildering transparency
how often does the fish give
thought to the
water it's
in

Being & Time

being
here is
easy but doing
something with it now that's
another story which sometimes requires
recourse to an earlier map retracing
that not so travelled exacting path of his
early thinking slow going generative for
the pilgrim's staff in hand making
a deliberate new way to play
the resurrected tune of
thinking it
through

the second telling of the story is identical to the first only this time supposedly the upshot is that the prisoner cannot free himself from the prison & i think of course he can it happens all the time or more accurately it happens every now & then but the critical element of healing is the presence of another human being those near dying live in another country we think we do but we do not like within the same sense of time perfectly fine then to listen to the cadence & music of a language that you do not understand it doesn't matter as long as our hearts are directed toward turn determined turn & turn without your original receipt you will face trouble at the return counter though no one can say who made up these strict & unreasonable policies teshuvah a returning to or i am weeping for all this perfection for the beauty of this instant being transmuted into its disappearance there it goes just around the corner on earth fading into it the talmud my friend is full of many such stories in the hospital on the page on the meditation cushion at the window in bed at night 23 were in a perfect radiant world who knew it if we just could see it could find & sing its intimate music *

2/4/07

the second telling of the story
is identical to the first only this time   supposedly the upshot is
that the prisoner cannot free himself from the prison   i think of course he can   it
happens all the time   or more accurately   it happens every now & then
but the critical element of the

healing   is the presence of another
human being   those near dying live in another country
we think we do but we do *not* live within the same sense of time   perfectly fine then to
listen to the cadence & music of a language you do not
understand   it doesn't matter   as

long as our hearts are directed
toward   turn determined turn & turn   without your
original receipt you will face trouble at the return counter   though no one can say
who made up these strict & unreasonable policies
teshuvah   a returning *to*   or

i am weeping for all this
perfection   for the beauty of this instant   being
transmuted into its disappearance   there it goes   just around the corner   on
earth   fading into it   the Talmud my friend is full of
many such stories   in the

hospital   on the page   on
the meditation cushion   at the window   in
bed at night   we were in a perfect radiant world   who knew it   if
we just could see it   could find   & sing
its intricate music

3/11/07

& why is it   that so much of being
turns away from us   remains steadfastly beyond or
beside our awareness   one day as a small child she
stopped to say "you know   water does not have much
taste"   & so it is with being   though each *does*
have a specific local momentary taste   & each *is*
absolutely crucial   the difficulty is attuning to

that taste to
develop slowly over
a life time
a feel for
being as we
are water spiders
moving upon that
surface tension up
held or birds
living within the
governing air it
is every where
beneath & around
us we are
each its particular

instance incarnate exemplification
signature fingerprint genetic
determination none of
this gets to
the heart of
it   dog spins
round chasing its
tail to make
a comfortable protective
bed in underbrush
i sit still
in what is

3/24/07

here is where

it begins with

her with Linda[1]

who taught me or more accurately got me to read

philosophy at first Kierkegaard & Nietzsche with pleasure

& large amounts of incomprehension as in viewing a

a painting or attending

a dance event

being & time

an abiding pleasure in its slow unfolding no doubt

a consequence stemming from that initial invitation

forty years ago & Stan[2] now many years into

his pursuit of

Biblical Hebrew we

with great

joy stumbled upon together *memra* the radio voice

of god a sporadic transmission enter then a

passioned protected wireless network tap into the

invisible omnipresent juice

film for a year:

who walks by

the back door of the frame shop the specifics of their

1 Linda Goodman, my aunt, graduated in philosophy from Reed College.
2 Stan Goodman, my uncle (mother's brother) – in early stages of Alzheimer's/dementia.

gait   the light at that moment   the stack of blue

& red containers across the alley way   *tikkun* *tikkun*

clicking in your

mouth   *tikkun* *tikkun*

taking part in

the necessary repair of

find it in first light or

deliberate attention to breath   *kadosh*   *kadosh*

notation   that *ruach*   that breath was given

& you

take it

from there

it's all a matter of what happens perhaps a life

time of preparation for five minutes of writing

for you who see or read or hear this   it will be

something different   the terms of your world having changed

the enigmatic figure of the dancing man dancing

in the doorway   dancing in defiance   in pure grace

3/25/07

y'is g'dal
you're such a doll

to care to care
tikkun tikkun

path among the happenstance

acacia
in case of

row row row your boat
rhododendron

azalea
assail ya

back home we don't

that death would dress a little bit gothic

& look & act somewhat like a distracted valley girl

upright piano
encased
in a
massive block of ice

chip away my little sister play Misty for me

4/22/07

& the odd

purpose of the poem

same is true

for being & time

it is as

john cage said it

the highest purpose

is to have no

purpose poem being

time reflecting one another

each being un

determined & having every

determination to remain

so thinking the pure

pleasure cat asleep

on the rail of

the deck aglow

in the sunset that

each thing is

each person in time

each bathed in

an unapparent invisible being

nothing at all

added by these names

5/21/07

that mortality may not be a necessary condition of the
human
& if such change primordial formative were
to occur whether rebellion against an unforgivable disobedience
or fulfillment of the divine as we partake of it
we would
begin then a new set of relations to being & time
what
to say in conversation with myself
wherein the dead
live & speak take turns looking through these reconstituted
eyes
each day first to bury the immediate dead
to honor those in transition

6/13/07

hacking kaballah
black fire white fire
word-word letter-letter

rise and enter the city
and you will be told what
you are to do

among the many words
searching in time

called out of
                    or called into
call it a calling
                    i'm here calling
on you (a cold call) because i have been
called upon to do so

6/14/07

how to answer back

to what cannot be seen or heard

6/16/07

again the dead

return

propelled by memory

process of familiar

names

Manya Fanya Sonia[3]

Chaim   a secret

name

a history of

exchanging names Esau

misspelled

Essa somehow becomes

Chuck   & Chaim

becomes

Grandpa Butchie   between

name & thing

between

name & person

some chasm ornate

as

any illustrated manuscript

3 Brief story of family names: my mother's mother, my father's mother, my mother's mother's sister, my father's father; Essa was my father's given name, though he ended up being called Chuck and Charles was his official name.

what a smile

which

goes to the

heart of human

being

a pure smile

radiates whatever energy

is

consonant with us

7/24/07
Asheville NC

over the years there came a series of us & we were
writing & thinking what mattered was the sporadic
thread of our gratitude & the beautiful complexity
of its uniquely established structure world &
poem a Talmud in process the work of the 36
finding a way to uphold & augment what is

i read yesterday about a 111 year old man
schizophrenic poor hard working a patient in town
in the state mental hospital if left to his
own devices each day he would stretch out
a long sheet of brown butcher paper & draw
intricate large homes & farm scenes with pink

chickens & blue cows trees clouds tractors
he had always worked hard a poor black
man living on the gorgeous sequestered rundown
grounds of Bryce Hospital now & then pulled
away from his drawing to go bowling or swimming
or to join the other patients for a simple meal

Tangible, they tell
the reassurances,
the comforts,
of being human.[4]
of what must be spoken
to inspire   as breath   as spirit   given in the spirit of

i heard you   Bob   say these words   your words
you had written them   the words not yours   the
odd staccato specific twist   the turning of them
yours   heard you say them   twenty-eight years
ago   not too far from here   & had then

no idea what would open up   an energy
& passion toward something i might be   but
what is young enthusiasm   & who can possibly
tell which circulation becomes a rushing river
canyon   & an active & engaging way   as

you would say   or said   *onward*

it is a mystical thing   to be found here now

---

4 Robert Creeley, "Love," *Selected Poems*, Berkeley: UC Press, 1991, p. 233.

half a life ago
            & odd
                        or not at all
to be here
            again
                        to stumble upon
as by chance
            "there are words voluptuous
                        as the flesh"
words that have
            a life that
                        give or make
possible a way
            difficult & dignified
                        to proceed
voluptuous then
            in their own way
                        we hold them &
say them   words
            "Not to speak them
                        makes abstract
all desire
            and its death at last"
                        these words
& their life
            in time with
                        odd determination

giving to us

if we attend

all that they are

which is

in fact

what we are

2/17/08

was   time   in story is   again

though never

as it was

for example

when my parents in 1971 moved from San Jose to the Monterey Peninsula   but wait   let me back up a little   for a number of years they had done decently with their real estate business that is until they sold a home (in our neighborhood) to a black family & the neighbors   led by a family friend & a member of the Temple   blocked the sale   over the next year or two nothing overt or dramatic happened but their real estate business dried up & they stopped getting listings from the Jewish community & it became clear that they were going to have to make a change   my father looked at various businesses & eventually chose to buy a liquor store in Seaside just outside the Fort Ord Army Base   for a few months my mom stayed behind in San Jose while my dad worked on the liquor store & then they moved to a house in the Del Monte Forest in Pebble Beach   when they told Manya (my mother's mother) that they were moving to Pebble Beach her response was simple & direct: "what   in the forest with the goyim?!"   and no doubt she pictured a grim repetition of what had happened to her own family during the pogroms in Russia fifty or sixty years earlier   i imagine she pictured Cossacks on horseback storming my parents' house in Pebble Beach

Fanya (my father's mother) on the other hand reacted to the news of the move quite differently   for twenty years my family including aunts uncles cousins grandparents had all lived within walking distance of each other & a move by anyone even to another part of town was a big deal   so when my father told Fanya about the impending move to Pebble Beach she asked "did you steal anything?"   my father was shocked   was quiet for a moment   & then said "no"   to which Fanya said "then if it doesn't work out you can always move back"

Fanya's grasp of English was never the best   when my sister Terri in high school had been sick for a couple of weeks   fever aches tired all the time   & the doctor finally did a blood test & figured out what was wrong i remember my mother calling Fanya to tell her "Terri has mononucleosis" & after a long pause   Fanya asked "is it good for the Jews?"

7/14/08
San Miguel de Allende

if

the world

& it does

presents intersection

with the words you

may know *desayuno* *demasiado*

in your given language & perhaps

one or two others what

if there is a fork

in the road

ser &

estar

sein zion sign design sigh

estar a star esther the dancer

7/17/08

San Miguel de Allende

not i
love you
i love
space in
which you
are fact
that you
are &
so in
visible in
your par
ticulars
engen
dering
or en
gine of
entire
conver
sations
time given
to read
the in
direct
love of
inter
mittent
turn &
return

7/24/08

the message says

    he[1] died of natural causes

        what does that mean

a seizure at age 32

    i see him in the bardo

        black hat enigmatic smile

still working on his music &

    his paintings & all pain

        has fallen away   Zorn

warbles & shrieks on the sax

    & the Pak-being has his

        most recent life washed

away so to re-enter time

    with the full force of his

        chaos embracing love

---

1 Pak Nichols, outsider (or self-taught) artist and musician; at 33 years old, he died in Montgomery, Alabama. He was a former student of mine, and we collaborated on a series of nine poem-paintings. For more about Pak, see http://www.marciaweberartobjects.com/nichols.html

9/8/08

odd music the music of time dividing
time into intervals of exploratory sense
sense of time as a way into being as
a way to sense being as it is only
in time music amusing or arousing
causing being & time to be for a
moment palpable as music as the
recurrence a watery currency call it
water music the page the barge upon
the river mark it remark upon it
where you are music mark it with an X

12/24/08

what is said then in the immediate afterward
& thereafter is elegy
whether by name or not
as the kaddish never mentions death

she she the shekinah
beloved unto the father
beloved unto the mother
beloved unto the sister & the brother

what thou lovest well i gave her all my love
where does it go it doesn't go at all
call now to no response
not true not true at all the books were futile

we never addressed this
we had no need to
i will go as far as *cho fu sa*[2]
if it is there that i might see you

2 Cf. Pound's "The River-Merchant's Wife: A Letter."

2/8/09

seeking work

in a world

that barely exists

how the word   cancer   changes everything

that we are given

the right problems

in the right amount

that the gap of pain

opens up

an inrushing

of love

From *Thinking in Jewish (N20)* (2017)

2/12/11

It takes a while to settle into the pages of the book
to settle into the being of the book it takes
an odd kind of leisure

hours a winter morning before anyone else is awake
ice slowly melting on the dead
hydrangea blooms

"We understand that shapes or forms pour into and out of being, while something subsists." <70>

aura to under
stand when each word is transit transitory door
way each word attended to surpassing understanding a winter morning

"... the there is, which wounds less than disappearance does" <70>

3/1/11

"There is in pure being, then, nothing to think." <74>

don't worry, it's nothing

" Nothingness

runs

through

being."

<75>

"Time is pure hope. It is even the birthplace of hope." <96>

"The fear of dying is the fear of leaving a work unfinished." <101>

"y'all need to cut y'all's lights on bright"

in the region of the possible where we think we have work to do his work is done

i saw his last breath drew an entire community into that mystery

spoke it & spoke it only once said what the spirit moving through had to say

some had been said in the dream some had a first life

in thinking in conversation

it is also what makes him think

musical

3/14/11

3/27/11

round is round reading around one day one morning a gray day crepe myrtle putting forth first leaves of spring dogwood beginning to blossom sounds of a possible storm rocking around if you come across it a passage everything changes in motion i am still i am still in motion but for how long

5/9/11

adonai echad

we are

beings uniquely placed in language a language we had no hand

in making

"after the glimpse of holiness, which is primary" <ix>

shin ku myo u
from true emptiness,
the wondrous being appears
<55/109>

6/8/11
6/10/11

such great pleasure in
so musical such pleasure adventure
such is the pleasure in attending

in joy to awaken to the
beginning with the sweet in-
such great pleasure in sitting

in love with the small miracle
this day to wear the prayer shawl
to say it & to sing it

"or the preliminary necessary to awakening" <26> who study
this curriculum of the soul "as if God could abide with-
in me" <26> in the form of our love of the world "as
though the adventure of cognition were not all of the spirituality
of thought, as if it were rather the falling asleep of a wake-
fulness!" <27> witness the energy of attention "rather of
reanimating – or of reactivating – this life" <27> & put on the
prayer shawl "as though consciousness fell asleep in 'being
awakened' to things" <27> yes of course it is here now & now

learning to think being
in finding this feeling for being
to being's infinite variations
numbered threads
finity of language & music

still wide awake this morning
of each breath its complex conversion
to finger its many comforting threads
quietly to yourself

yes give this machine a rest
oh my son my only son so good to hear your voice so far away
in this rain the gray machinery of time
this language that they say is mine is not
what am i native to if not the question
a thing which has/which is its own time a questionable being
without announcement
you & i
are
simply here
what else
could we have been
waiting for
nothing
absolutely nothing

< for glenn >

7/23/11
Edinburgh

slow awakening from stone from stone structures from the cunning corridors from the dates & names once again a vision of the beloved once again dissolving in time

from hillside from overlook from swan-shaped rock pulpit in air from transept & nave

“It wakes thought up” [66]

9/22/11
honolulu

who comes to mind that is this place that is this time that comes to mind

feel the swell & take it home

at each turning turn &

turn so it may be swell & take it home

& thinking here of thee & sing those on the horizon

of his singing each turn it is a yearning feel the

"for to believe is precisely this dialectical wavering" (2017)

returning for one & know the horn the given instrument

instrumental in our singing what comes to mind take a turn feel the swell & take it home

for another & know the making of the book is the given instrument

feel the swell & take it home

10/8/11
shabbat
yom kippur

שבת
is

is a palace in time
so it comes to mind
an oasis refuge
is a portal for knowing time through rest in time

"rather than space" (AJH,10)
tied to this measure" <123>
sacred moments" (AJH,6)

is: then it comes to mind
a ray of light of light that stays
beginning with the end of daylight

"deaf to information, indifferent to the confirmations" <123>

sabbath as to celebrate time

"Is the thought going toward God"

"and thus to discover meanings that did not rejoin being" <122>

to face

"The result of our thingness is our blindness to all reality that fails to identify itself as a thing, as a matter of fact.
This is obvious in our understanding of time, which, being thingless and insubstantial, appears to us as if it had no reality." (AJH,5)

so dark so soon where ted has gone before the darkest part of year so dark so soon the light arrives by faith

in turning the small space where i am quiet one who speaks a sudden song & makes the singing great

archway over the dark day

arriving into light

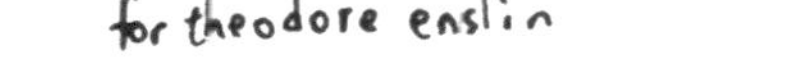
for theodore enslin

d. 11/22/11

12/16/11

i am not the angel singing i listen to what the angel sings yes the angel sings i am not the angel singing i, with my eyes, right hand this is ongoing

Fine, I said. Firmament.

"I call bullshit on firmament. There's no such thing as firmament."

There is, though, I said, It's in Torah.

"What's it mean, then?"

I said, No one really knows what it means. In Hebrew, it's the place where Adonai resides, but it's a bad translation. It's really more like border — it's confusing.

"I don't think that's fair," she said. "If you don't know what it means, you can't use it."

That's your rule, I said. I said, That's not my rule.

<The Instructions, 104>

angel sings

"I have given you to write"

3/24/12

2021 days

"To answer 'הנני' means that you give the Hay (ה) of your being over to the One who calls" <34/Kushner/Book of Letters>

having gathered in the word

הנני

"in which, in the adventure of a possible holiness, the human interrupts the pure obstinacy of being as war of." <233>

this would be / is

as it is

without end

"like a preface to possible research" <233>

here i invite you to be

From *Evidence of Being Here: Beginning in Havana (N27)* (2018)

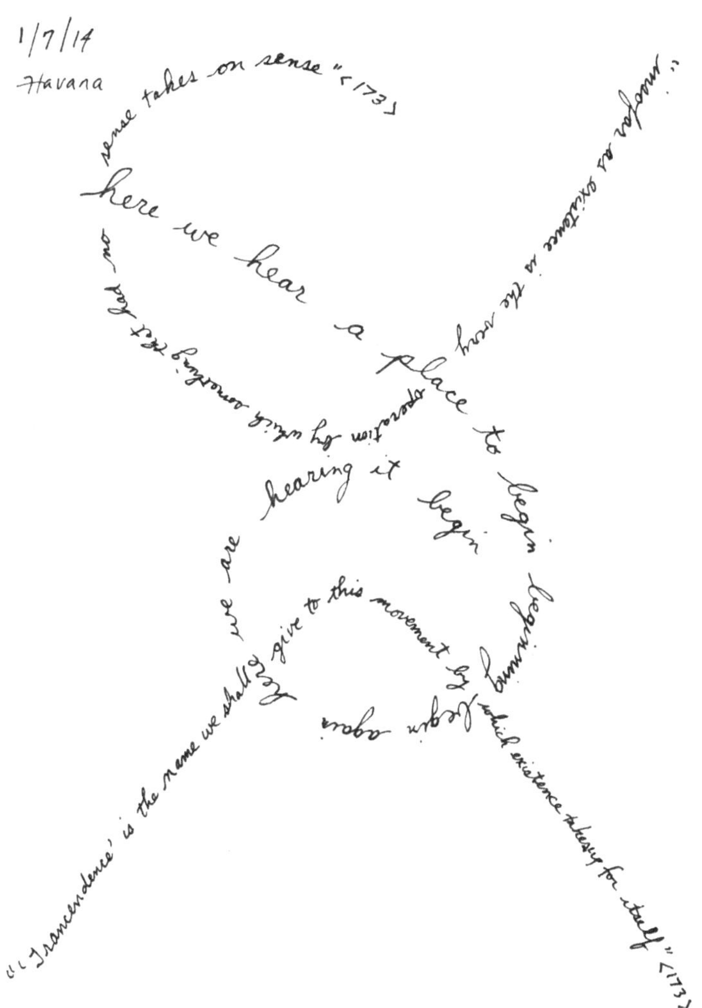
1/7/14
Havana
here we hear a place to begin
we are hearing it begin
beginning begin again
"insofar as existence is the very operation by which something yet had no sense takes on sense" <173>
"'Trancendence' is the name we shall give to this movement by which existence taking for itself" <173>

1/17/14

ε, if in this way we are waiting

ε, if they may contact us ε, if they are

ε, if this is the best way we can inquire as it is the way we have been given

ε if you come to know it in the strange way it may be known

rain down softly the light caress

"I relate to the word just as my hand reaches for the place on my body being stung." <186>

"but rather an effort to reopen time" <1877>

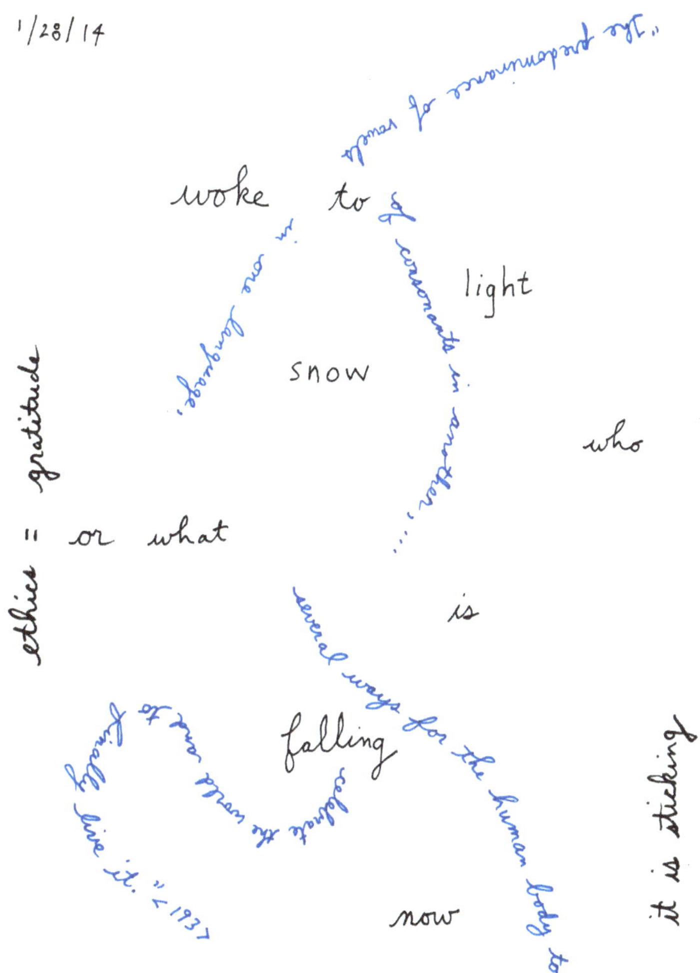
1/28/14
woke to
light
snow
who
is
falling
now
it is sticking
ethics = gratitude
or what
"The predominance of vowels
in one language,
of consonants in another, ...
several ways for the human body to
celebrate the world and to
finally live it." ~1937

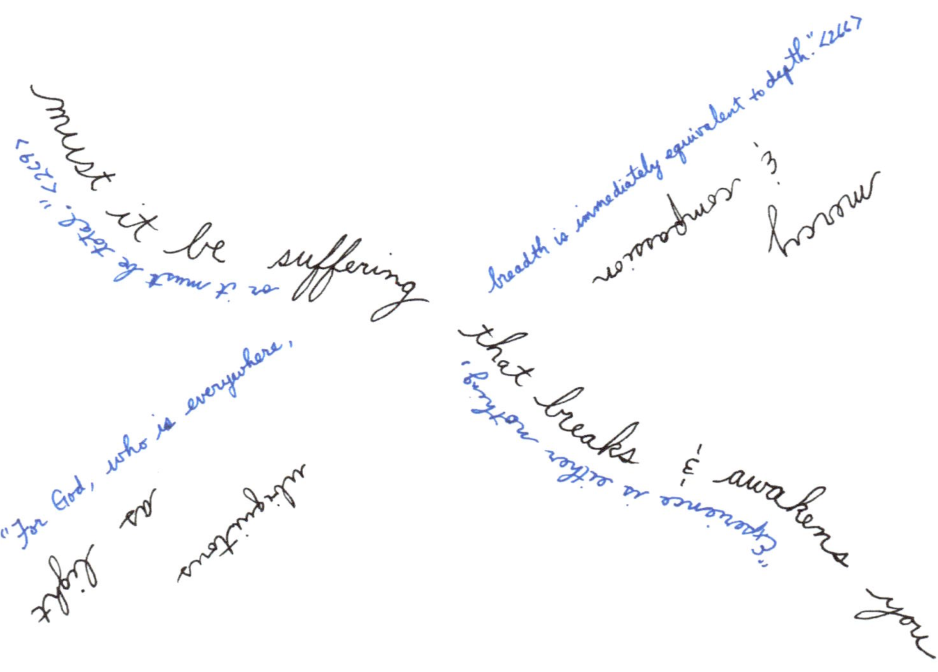
must it be suffering
that breaks & awakens you
"Experience is either nothing,
or it must be total." <269>
mercy & compassion
breadth is immediately equivalent to depth." <266>
"For God, who is everywhere,
ubiquitous
as light

4/1/14

i have written a wisdom book
lost in a larger book &
hidden from myself if i
would find it i
must do as you
would do i must
read it again &
listen to what it
is saying & then
shall we
extract it
or simply let it
remain hidden

“. . . to ask experience for its own sense,
in a word, phenomenology.” <2305>

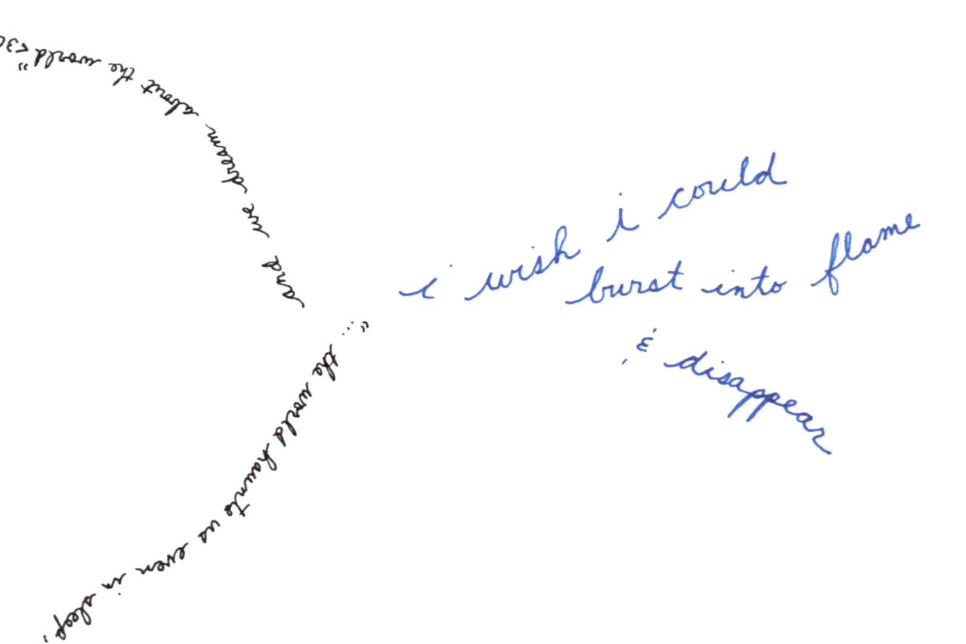
i wish i could
burst into flame
& disappear
:: the world haunts us even in sleep,
and we dream about the world" <306>

4/10/14
diamond head

here what do you say within this flow of words you hold your own

does not also increase

whether one's distance from them

4/13/14
diamond head

planning or having a strategy
for when things get worse
a couple in their eighties
thinking rationally thinking proactively
where & near what & near whom
& the cost & how long & what
levels of care & sharing this
thinking with their children
while visiting together while
enjoying a thai meal in a
hole in the wall restaurant
in kaimuki not directly
a talk about death but rather
pleasure great pleasure and attention
to the almost perfect sauce
of the evil jungle prince

"But this can only be a manner of speaking, for we do not know our body or the power, weight and shape of our organs,
like an engineer knows the machine he has assembled piece by piece." [328]

4/16/14
Tuscaloosa

"It is not consciousness who touches or who palpates, it is the hand, and the hand is, as Kant says, 'man's outer brain.'" [330]

where or when
will
consciousness
ever be
at
home

4/24/14

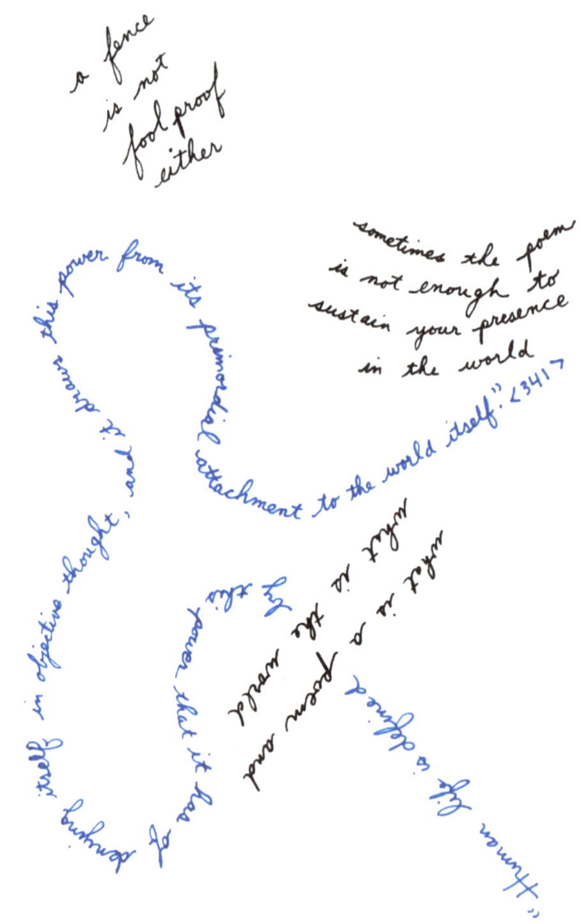
a fence
is not
fool proof
either
sometimes the poem
is not enough to
sustain your presence
in the world
"Human life is defined
by this power that it has of denying itself in objective thought, and it draws this power from its primordial attachment to the world itself." <341>
what is the world
what is a poem and

From *Slowly Becoming Awake (N32)* (2019)

6/1/16

the empty form is really not

i suppose i am writing &   it is not the sun   & not a sphere neither

i first came upon the clearing while sitting & attending to my breathing

it has nothing of the narrative about it

cog   said the old   codger

cogitate

think   it over

"For example, how about the words, 'I have attained the way simultaneously with sentient beings on the great earth'?" <216>

isn't this where you left off

cogitate

the empty form is really not

i first came upon the clearing while sitting & attending to my breathing

it has nothing of the narrative about it

cog said the old codger

i suppose i am writing & it is not the sun & not a sphere neither

think it over

"For example, how about the words, 'I have attained the way simultaneously with sentient beings on the great earth'?" [216]

isn't this where you left off

6/1/16

6/7/16

can you tell me

what you will be thinking

five minutes from now

"consciousness & its objects"   the little things

reassuring us   that we are here

c o n s e n s u a l

r e a l i t y

taking off in any direction   ***after all***

"Thus, know that a true expression is not done by sound or form,

and a true teaching

has no particular shape." <245>

& what is that threshold

where matter

that has already been in being

begins to

experience consciousness

6/7/16

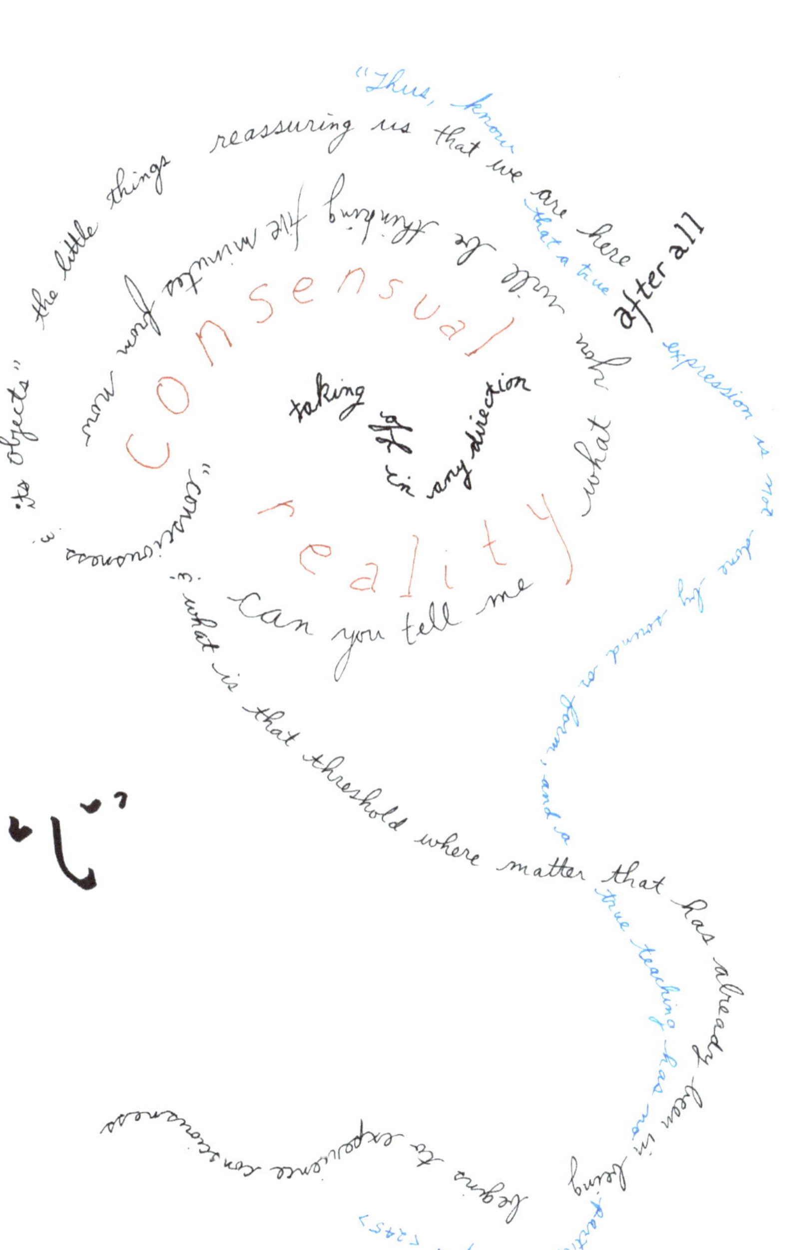

6/11/16

“One solid rail of iron
is the bird’s path.” <251>
as in the yiddish saying,
“burdens are from god, & shoulders also”
none escape the suffering
destined to be with you
it takes up residence within you
its exact nature
changing you from within

“Those who are shaken by death
and try to avoid it
are outside the way.” <253>

(Note: On June 18, 2016, I fell very ill and spent the next 26 days in the hospital, losing 35 lbs., making two trips to the ICU, due to a diverticulitis infection that burst, creating many subsequent complications. It was the first time since my birth that I had spent any time in a hospital.)

6/11/16
Tuscaloosa

"One solid rod of iron is the bride's path." <254>

as in the yiddish saying, "burdens are from god, shoulders also." none escape the suffering destined to be with you it takes up residence within you its exact nature changing you from within

"Those who are shaken by death and try to avoid it are outside the way." <253>

永

9/7/16

Carrollton

it could be so

early day light shadows upon the hillside

cows drifting toward the tractor

after meditation   taking inventory of my aches & pains

today we'll unseal   the bids at   the lawyer's office to see the bids on Cooter's old farm equipment

what is a jew doing here

is that a voice

a friend in the distance

practicing vision

"If you inherit one phrase, you inherit mountains and you inherit waters. You cannot be separated from this place." <279>

mars saturn antares   invisible once again in the day sky

9/7/16
Carrollton

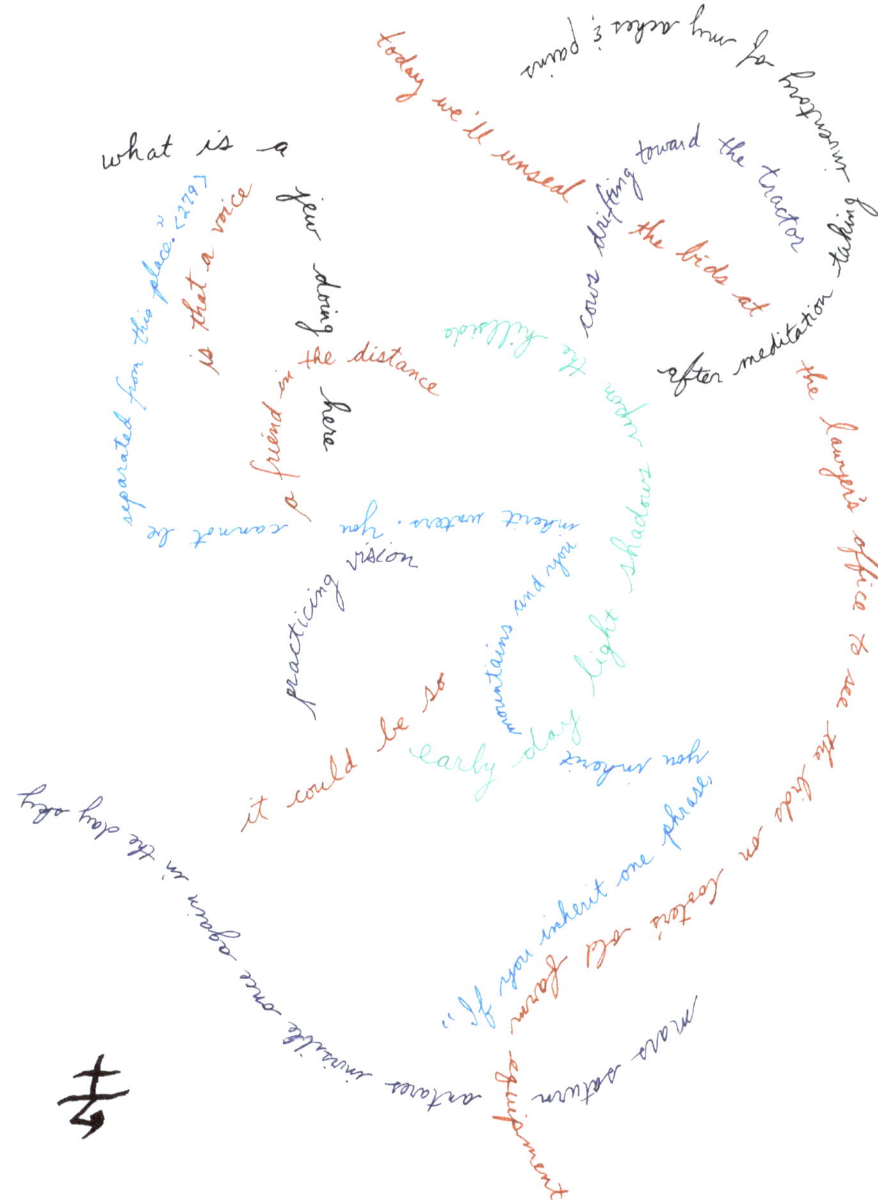

9/8/16

Tuscaloosa

& so we think of these things

& there we are   we are this very arising thinking arising & going away

"We say so because birth is itself perishing." <282>

& we turn that attention to this world – the ten thousand things –
& we see it there as we & our thinking are fully of it

9/8/16

Tuscaloosa

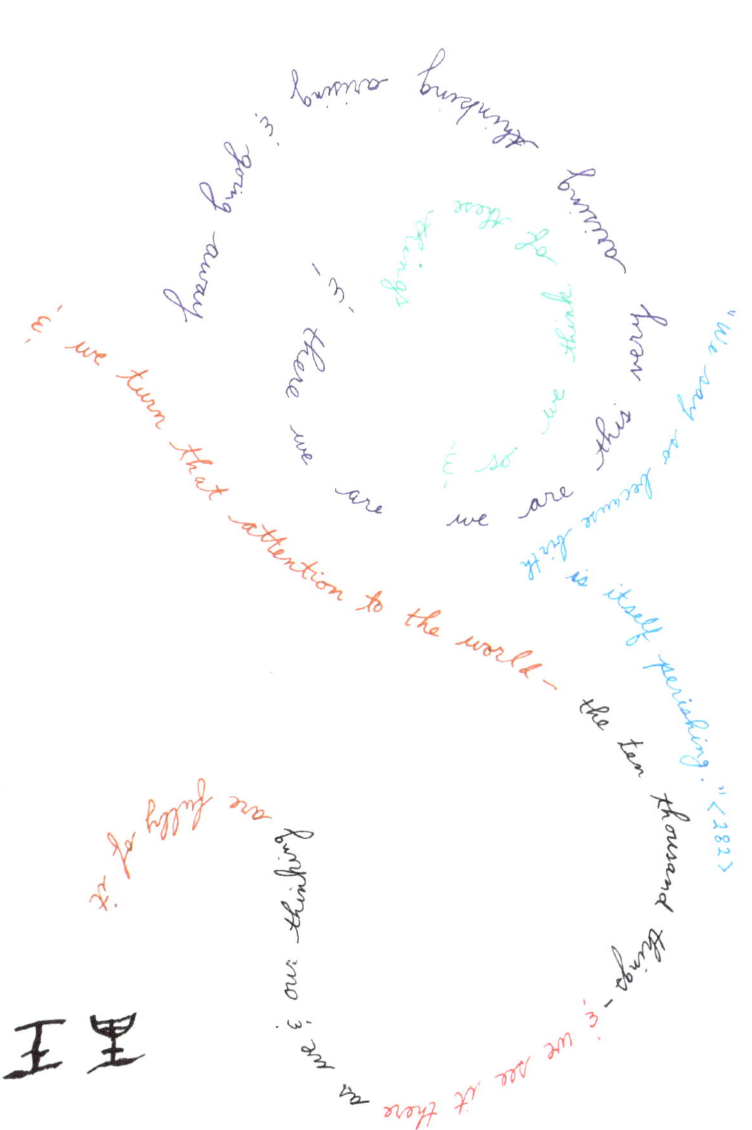

9/29/16

Carrollton

a golden dog

a black dog

& one i can't describe

came by shortly after dawn

came by the house

curious

sniffed around

ran down the hillside

crossed the gravel road

and disappeared

"There are also those who understand without teachers." <297>

9/29/16
Carrollton

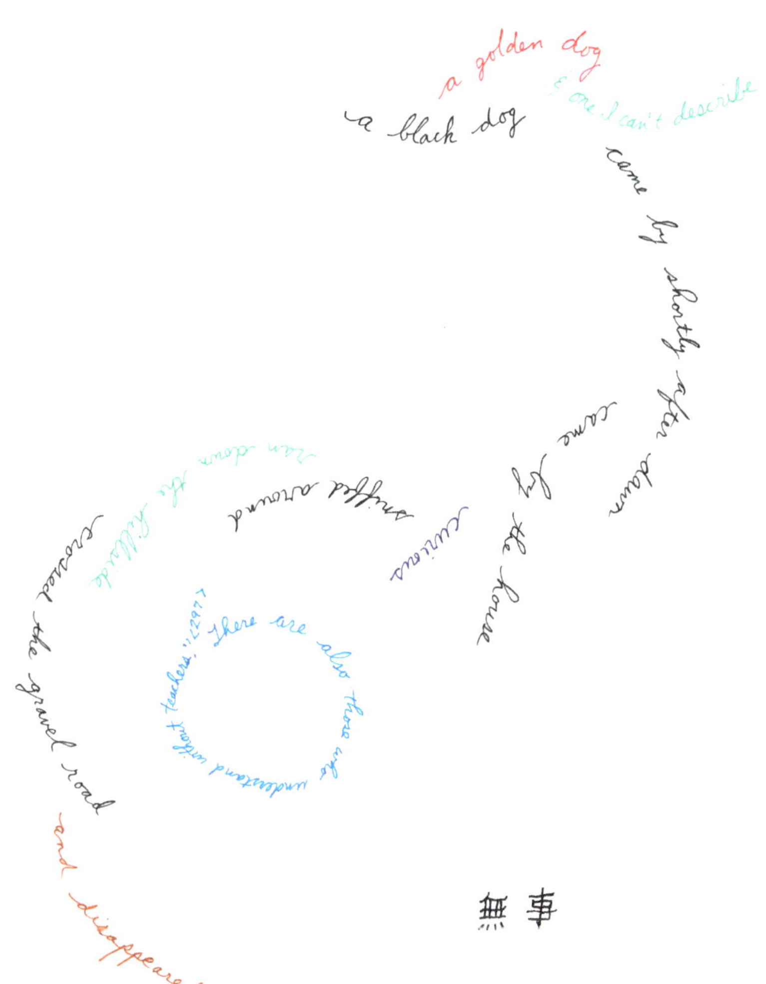

10/7/16

Carrollton

one

more

day

among

the sequence

of many

Lao Tzu as he left was asked to write it down

keep on reading keep on breathing

what

love with others

& the dogs

have their own

way of going

"If you say, 'I have become enlightened,'

you may suppose that enlightenment has a beginning." <301>

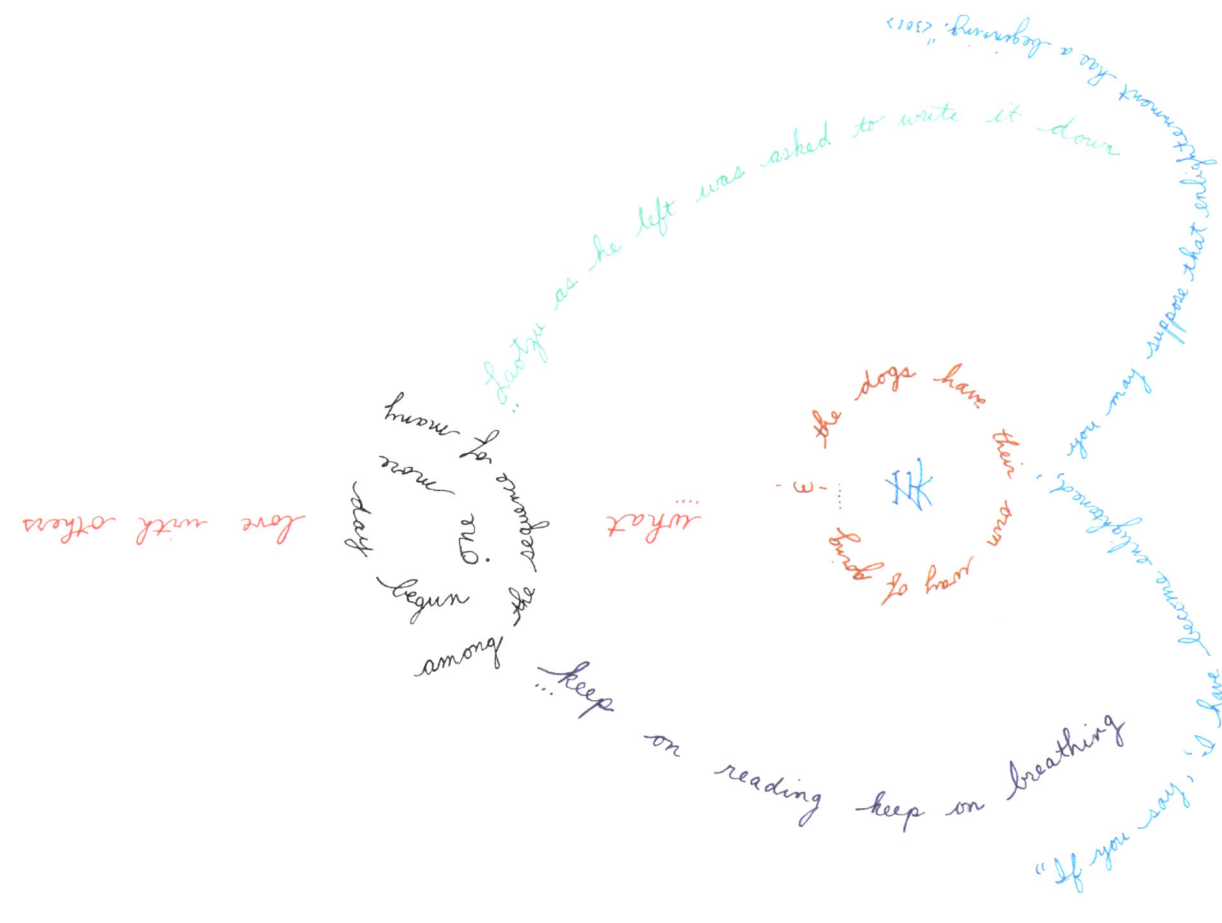

10/7/16
Carrollton

10/11/16
Cambridge (UK) Yom Kippur

reading now
once again
The New Spirit
there are phrases i would write differently
but
it is now 17 years later
& in truth
now is exactly what does the writing

i read my old book
& it is all yours

head heart hand
inscribing now
all in the name of is

as I recover from the illness that struck me down
forgive me lord for my judgment of others
let this year be a succession of days where the wondrous night sky shines in mind

forgive me lord when i lose sight of the miracle of being

once again in a coffee house portal different languages & background music a
cacophony of human yearning a restoration which is each moment when attended to

"Who are beginners? Are there any who are not beginners?" <304>

10/11/16
Cambridge UK
Yom Kippur

Once again in a coffee house ......

laughters & background music a cacophony of human yearning a restoration which is each moment when attended to

forgive me lord when i lose sight of the miracle of being .....

all in the name of it

reading now once again The New Spirit

there are phrases i would write differently but it is now 17 years later & in truth now is exactly what does the writing

& i read my old book & it is all yours

insulting new

head heart hand ..... vs i sorrow

portal effect

from the illness that struck me down

Are there any who are not

forgive me lord for my judgment of others

let this year be a succession of days where the wondrous night sky shines in prima

"Who are beginners? ... beginners?" <304>

世界

10/13/16

Cambridge

"Do not treasure or belittle what is far away, but be intimate with it.

turned

shot through

i am no where

dark nothing matter

more than here

chock full

down

we will turn the wheel together

say it

reading

Do not treasure or belittle what is near, but be intimate with it." <305>

10/13/16
Cambridge

"Do not treasure or belittle what is far away, but be intimate with it."

turned

i

shot

am

full

here

dark

nothing

no

matter

物

then

where

chock

now

through

down

we will turn

the wheel together

say it

reading

"Do not treasure or belittle what is near, but be intimate with it." 3057

11/5/16

Carrollton

they call them

fish bone clouds

even the body resists death

or especially

time in fragments

slow whitening of the sky

deer cautious at dawn along the tree line

L5 disc sending intermittent pain down my left leg

"Knowledge is a shape, and a shape is mountains and rivers." <312>

We sit on the front porch & he acts out his stories just below us

& maybe he tells us with a smile death is a welcomed rest who knows

& then there were four does & a young one ears fanned alert beside the cedar tree

"To maintain illumination is extraordinary and

to accept it as complete is no other than

doubting it thoroughly." <312>

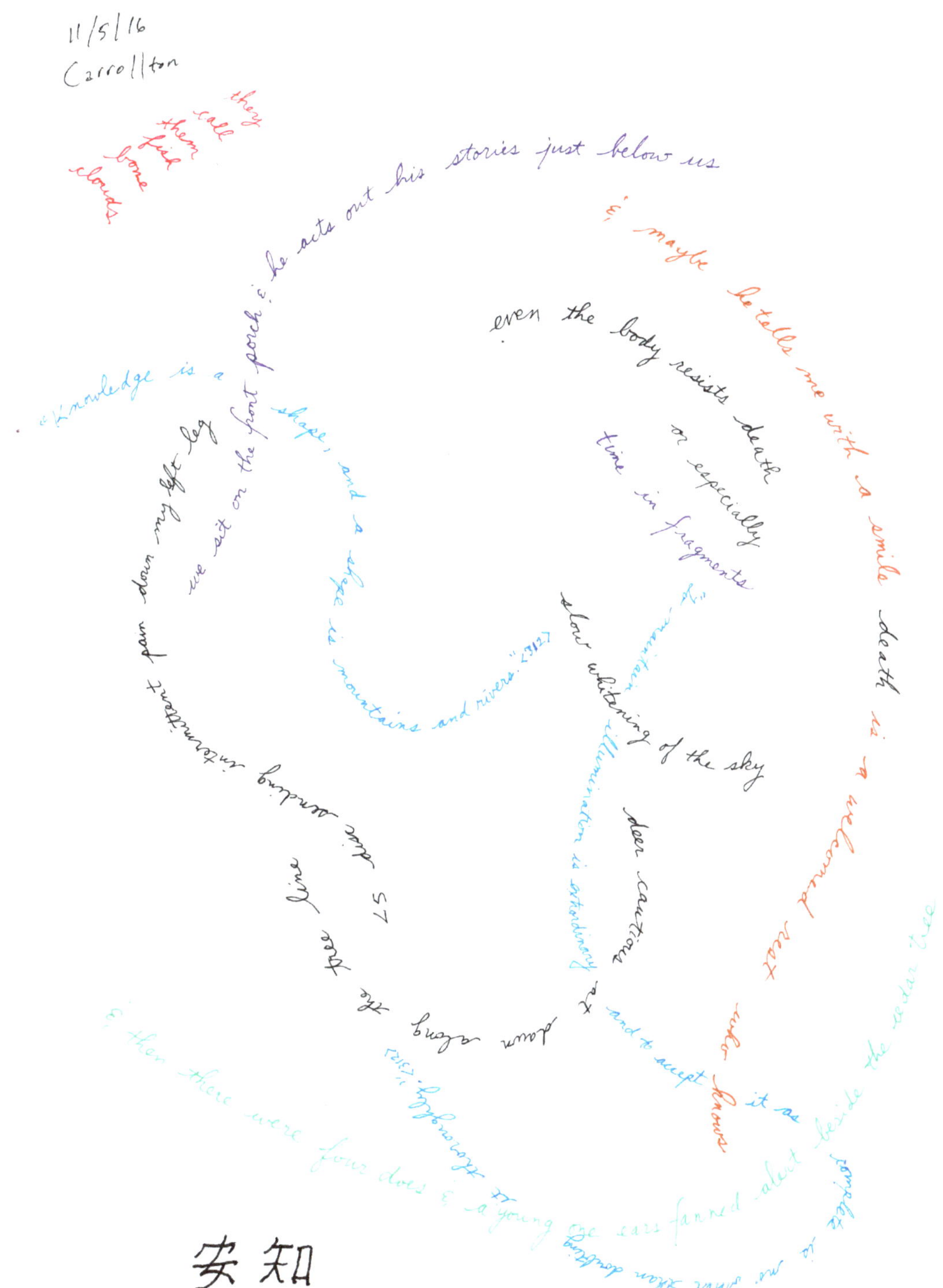
11/5/16
Carrollton
they call them fish bone clouds
we sit on the front porch & he acts out his stories just below us
& maybe he tells me with a smile death is a welcomed rest
who knows
even the body resists death
or especially time in fragments
"knowledge is a shape, and a shape is mountains and rivers." [312]
slow whitening of the sky
deer cautious & down along the tree line
L5 disc sending intermittent pain down my left leg
& sudden illumination is extraordinary and to accept it as complete is no other than doubting thoroughly." [312]
& then there were four does & a young one ears fanned alert beside the cedar tree
安知

1/7/17

"… enlightenment

& so to the sweetness of the new year

& so to the snow on the ground

exceeds

& so to the notion that every day is a beautiful day

the bound-

& so to seeing & knowing the beauty of immediacy

ary

& so to the sadness of the passing over of a dear friend

of the

& so to the blindness & mortality that awaits us

entire

& so to thank the other species that allow us to love them as pets

world. …

& so to the vastness of space beyond our comprehension

You know it because your body and mind are not you;
they appear in the entire world of the ten directions." <324>

1/7/17

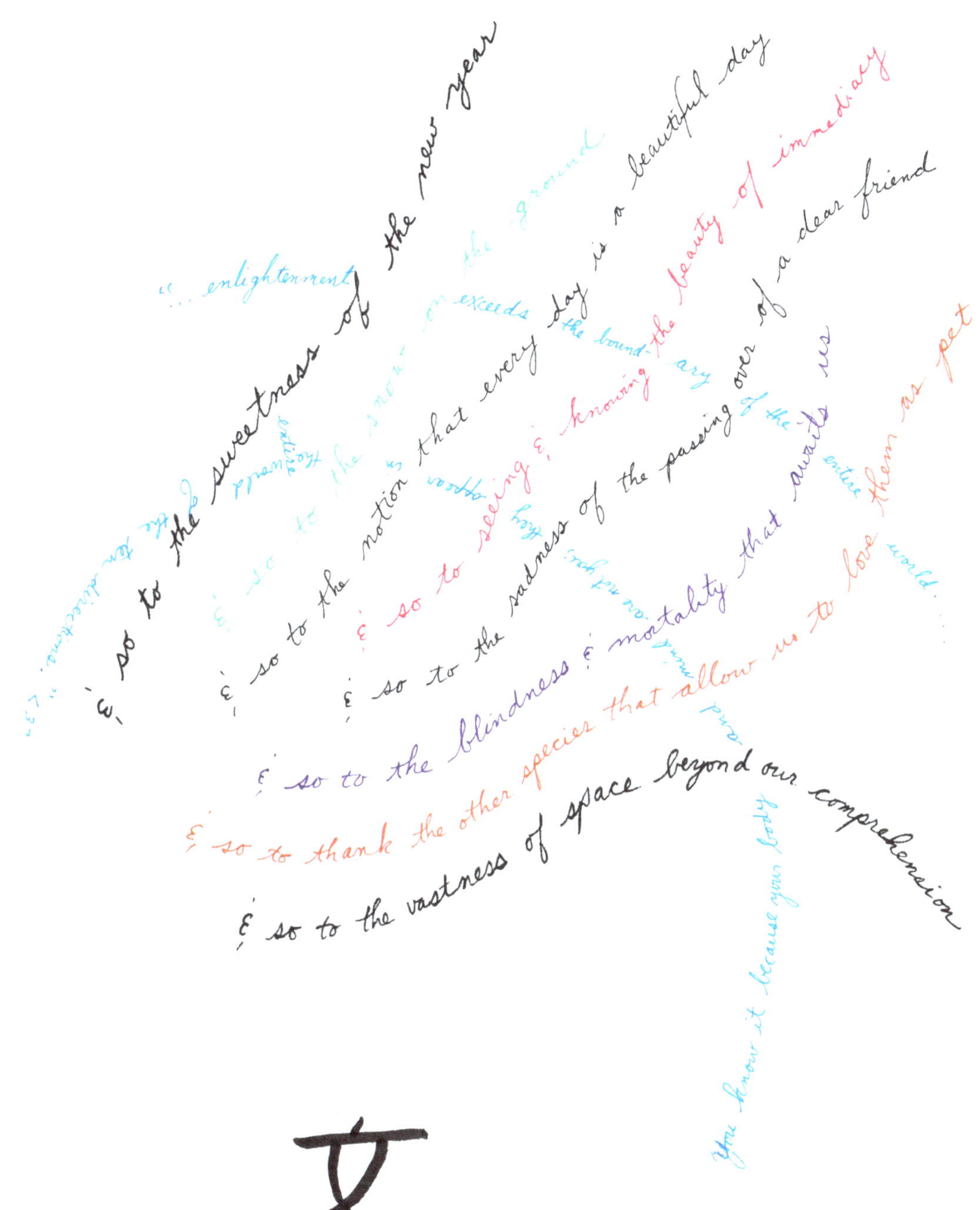

& so to the sweetness of the new year
& so to the snow on the ground
"... enlightenment exceeds the boundary of the entire world..."
& so to the notion that every day is a beautiful day
& so to seeing & knowing the beauty of immediacy
& so to the sadness of the passing over of a dear friend
& so to the blindness & mortality that awaits us
& so to thank the other species that allow us to love them as pet
& so to the vastness of space beyond our comprehension

1/9/17

what happens to

all our books

with their meticulous notes & markings

we had assumed

that someone would care

the words we have touched are

no more immortal

than we are

will every thing disappear

just as nothing disappears

"Your body is not you; your life is transported, moving in time without stopping even for a moment. …

The pure mind does not stay, it comes and goes in fragments. Even if there is truth,

it does not stay

within the boundary

of yourself." <325>

(in memory of William Doty)

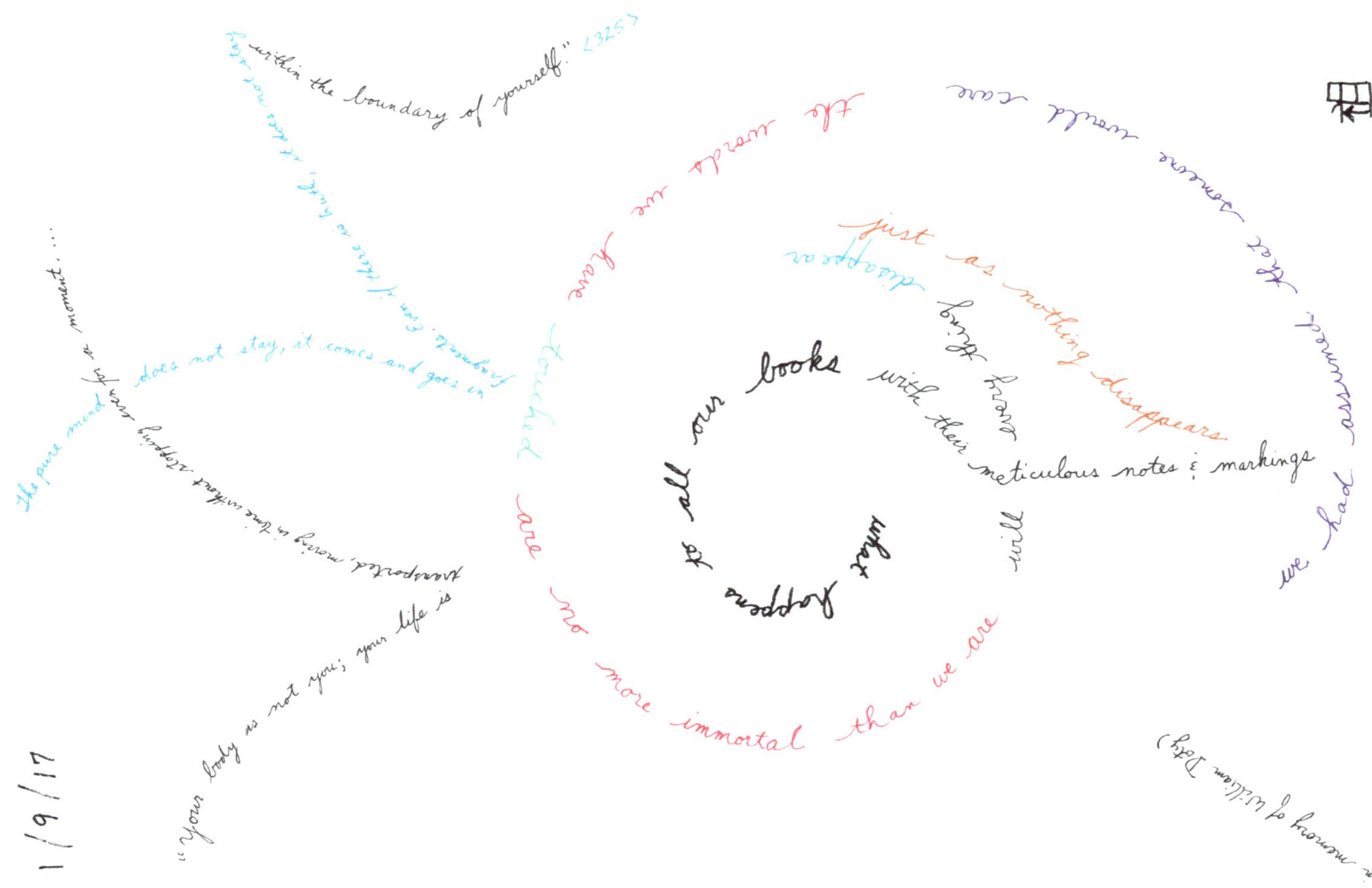

1/9/17
"Your body as not you; your life is transported, moving in time without stopping even for a moment. ...
The pure mind does not stay, it comes and goes in fragments. Even if there is truth, it does not stay within the boundary of yourself." ⟨325⟩
what happens to all our books with their meticulous notes & markings
we had assumed that someone would care
the words we have touched are no more immortal than we are
will every thing disappear
just as nothing disappears
(in memory of William Doty)

1/15/17

Carrollton

down
yonder
way

who

who gives from nothing

who labors here

at dawn bringing the cows a bale of hay

who

who knows each cow labors for them & would sell one for slaughter only with regret

who has chosen his work & is answerable to none

who will not leave & will not travel

who cleans away & burns the underbrush

holds his hand in front of the camera   & wants no picture made

to find a daily labor that is happiness

is there no grammar

that will name **this** a

work of art or love

“We should understand that the practice of the way

is no other than seeing into birth and death,

yet our practice is not bound by birth and death.” <336>

1/15/17
Carrollton

down
yonder
way

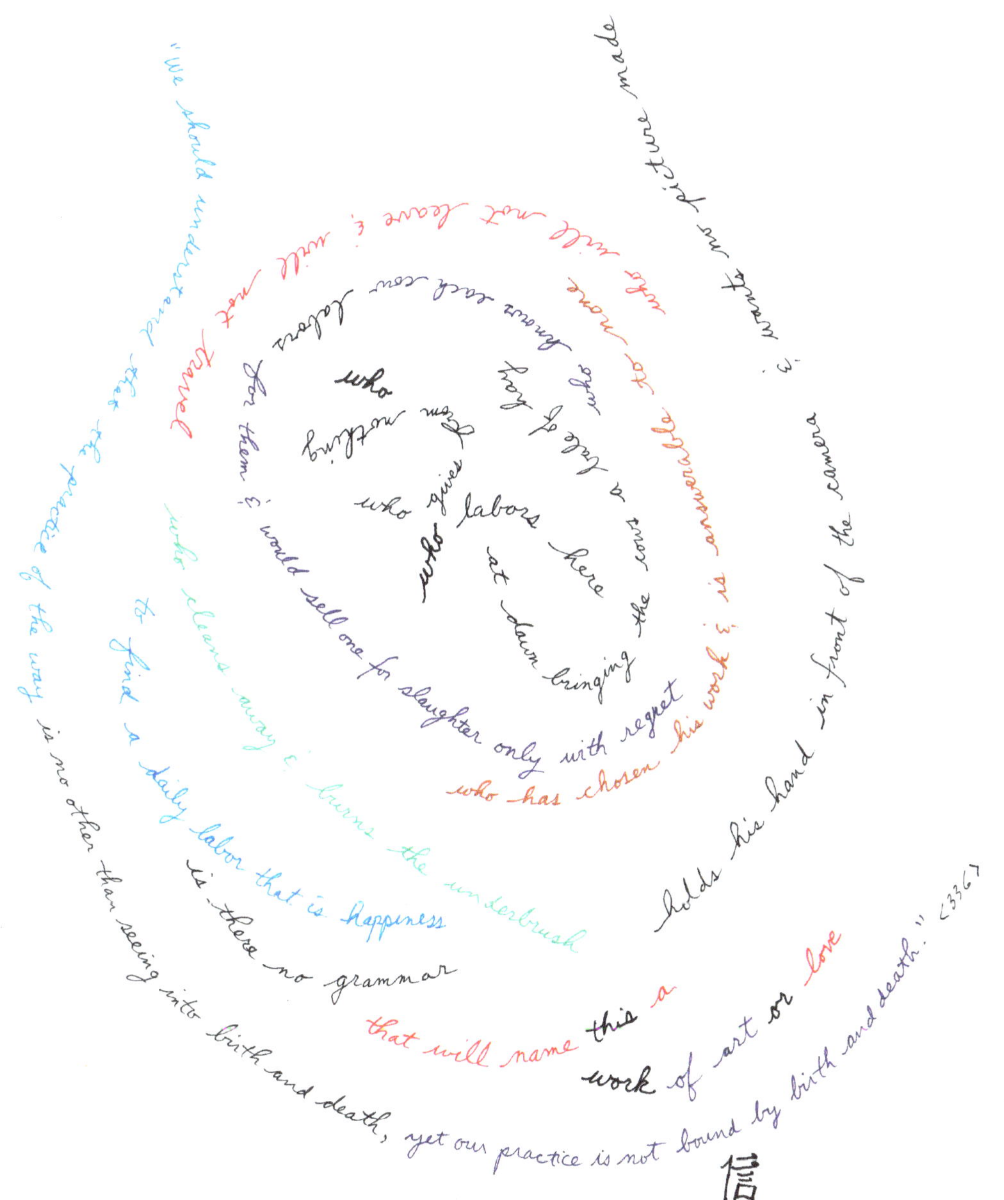

From *Poems That Look Just Like Poems* (2019)

As If

i begin
each day
(which is already
a false statement)
attending to my
study & the yard
the bird feeders
the weather
certain that this
simplified world
exceeds my under
standing of it
& so
that is how
& where
i begin
to write
words i re
turn to
as if
their appearance
were what i
was looking for

(5/20/14)

Already There

no need

to construct

an entry way into

language you are

already there

(or here)

call of hawk

circling above

second of the pair

circles nearby

Cooter takes his

oxygen tank with him

to the farm house

on the way points out to us

the home where he

& his brothers & sisters

were born

gravel roads pasture land

timber natural gas lines

Maybell looks in on him

two or three times a day

brings him some food

clarity

yes clarity above all

but what is it

& what is it to a man

living alone at eighty-seven

who has trouble

getting enough oxygen

(5/29/14)

Integrity

because it cannot
be taught
it matters
a way
of thinking
that refuses
to reduce thinking
to a set of learned
characteristics
because it can
not be other than
the infinite
complexity of
being itself
there is nothing
specific to be
learned nothing
to teach
& repeat
this is what
i mean by
pleasure
or
integrity

(6/3/14)

Infinite Light

after heavy rain
the infinite
light *namu amida*
butsu chanting softly
the buddha
of infinite light
walking the dogs
brother & sister
along a muddy
trail listening &
looking for deer
walking into &
through invisible
webs *namu*
amida butsu
dogs stop to
sniff a clump
of weeds
world of
information
in a few
days blue
berries will be
ripe the way
flows freely
through each

(6/13/14)

The Return

there is
a purity
upon the re
turn ask
jimmy giuffre
ask john zorn
ask george
oppen re
turn then to
a simplicity
or
call it
clarity that
for equally good
reasons
had been
resisted
ask bob
creeley ask
charles bernstein
or
to a purifying
emotion
so bare
in its exposure

that at its
root has
nothing
to do with
purity
which itself
is a dangerous
& impure
word

(6/27/14)

Close at Hand

we are given
mysteries
close at hand
the vessel
we live with
in
these
are the books
that can
teach us
the first
of these is
consciousness
which some
have called
the soul
how then
does a sub
stance that
does not think
rise into
thinking

(6/27/14)

Writing

do I know
what i am
writing
i
do not
how
you say
can this
be so
easy
try it
yourself
just begin
writing
with nothing
in mind

(7/28/14)

Brimming

it all
contributes
the bees
ardent in their
morning
labors
among beautiful
lavender
it does not matter
whether the teacher
remembers
to say so
impossible to say
what happened
in that first
second
what is
a moment
the body
eager
to dissolve
so we are
walking
with great
deliberation
brimming with

(7/29/14)

Moon

full moon
over
Santa Monica Pier
moon above
the illuminated
ferris wheel
a large scale
photo
now mounted
over his bed
in the assisted
living
facility where
he is dying
for several years
he had been
tracking
the coming &
going
of the full
moon
to take a photo
each month
one month
the moon

seen through
a Richard Serra
sculpture
the moon
became his way
of knowing
time
a cyclical
ritual
which he
performed
with great anticipation
& affection
until
he could
not
the moon
on the other
hand
continued
exactly
as it had

(8/18/14)

Who Is To Say

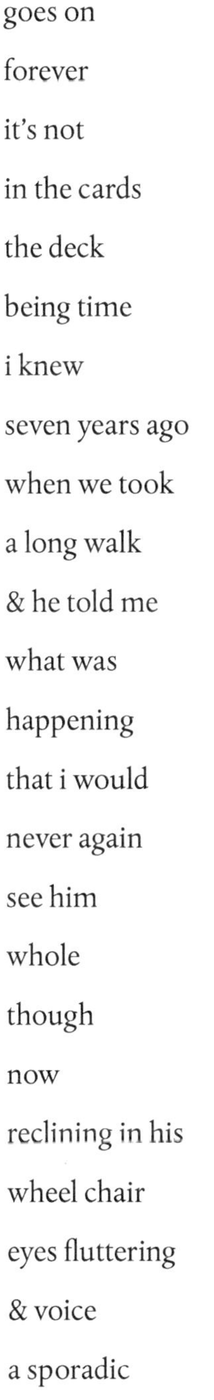

none of it
goes on
forever
it's not
in the cards
the deck
being time
i knew
seven years ago
when we took
a long walk
& he told me
what was
happening
that i would
never again
see him
whole
though
now
reclining in his
wheel chair
eyes fluttering
& voice
a sporadic

whisper
as he says
"shit,"
who is to say
he is not
fully there

(8/22/14)

Real Time

mourning
dove balancing
& bobbing
in the trapeze
platform
bird
feeder
early morning
after
meditation
the bird
& its motions
this is
the complete
story
of a mind
at work
or a mind
at play
cracking
open
the necessary
sun
flower
seeds

light &
shadow
from the pine
tree
a trace
of incense
what can
be
said
of the simultaneity
of being
hummingbird
coming to
the white
crepe
myrtle
blossom
beside
my study
window
what do
you
mean by
*"real
time"*?
is it
the male

cardinal

displacing

the mourning

dove

at the

bird

feeder?

(8/28/14)

The Picture of Being

as parents
are a perpetual
voice-over
whether living
or dead
i could not
draw you
a picture
of time
or
for that matter
of being
as my mother
whose own
mother
is invisible
still speaks
in a way
designed
to justify
to her mother
what she
does
& especially
what she

wants

the picture

of being

is only present

in these

words

if you

say them

but it all

boils down

to a matter

of need &

to live

makes no

requirement

that you think

about

being

time

though

is another

story

my mind

is

a dark sky

(8/29/14)

Oscar

a

point

of light

so far

away

if you

would

go there

you

could not

return

of course

there are

other

kinds of

beings

for whom

thought

is not

a compelling

condition

words

are not

best served

beholden

to some
didactic
wisdom
in fact
a moment
expands
as
the place
for an
aimless
& playful
transcription
if the new
black cat
oscar
keeps wandering
down that
gravel
pathway
into the
woods
will he
disappear

(10/11/14)

Sabbath

this morning
i am
at rest
hidden
beneath
a prayer
shawl
draped
over my
head
i am
chanting
your name
the un
pronounceable
one
something
indistinct
whispering
through
my lips
r u a c h
the breath
you
gave me

(10/18/14)

Radiant Gist

the conventional
sentiments
will do
just fine
but i must
say
that before
his brain
decayed
before faces
& names
went separate
ways
before
he could not
care
for himself
he found
the radiant
gist
of language
found it
in the ancient
hebrew
& aramaic

in the
taken apart
& studied
syllables
of one
particular
story
which became
his story
& in
a few
of the lesser
known
names
for the divine
& for a
while
he studied
& lived
& breathed
in that most
holy
place
in the slow
hard
earned
joy

of the study
of
torah
& he
spoke
& he
wrote
of the joy
of living
for moments
in that
profoundly
historical
radiant
language
where he
& those
prior
peoples
could dwell
in close
proximity
to
something
quite
beyond
us

something

that had

visited

him

too

through

the radiant

word

(11/2/14)

Head — Heart — Hand

Paris – March 16, 2016

the young rabbi
& i
we made a blessing
together
i had just
come back from
rouen
& i was
walking back
to my hotel
he stopped me
on my way
on rue des rosiers
& he asked me
are you jewish
& i said yes
& he asked me
to put on
the *tfillin*
said it would be
a mitzvah
for him
& i said
ok

& he asked me
if my mother's
family was jewish
on both sides
& i said yes
& he asked
if i had been
bar mitzvahed
& i said yes
& he was
surprised &
a little upset
that i had
never put on
the *tfillin* before
so we stepped inside
a little
laundromat
&
i took off
my overcoat
&
we put on
the *tfillin*
& we began
together
baruch

atah

adonai

& he told

me

that good things

would happen

this day

& as he

vanished

i told him

my few good words

of hebrew

kadosh

hashem

tikkun

&

teshuvah

Clanking

my vision is not
the child's
song of innocence
nor is it the one
of wonder my vision
is the insistent
voice of hypothesis
what if   what if
& a song
given over to
what is
for which i give
gratitude
in this vision
most of the thinking
is nothing but thanking
the clanking of a
language
released from its
chains

(11/23/14)

Bell

you are the bell
that awakens me

to said sound
& its dissolve

i am
written &

dropping back into
silence

leave space
for you

the sound of the bell
is the light of the day

(4/9/17)

From *COVID19 SUTRAS* (2020)

You have gained the pivotal opportunity of human form. Do not use your time in vain. You are maintaining the essential working of the buddha way. Who would take wasteful delight in the spark from the flintstone? Besides, form and substance are like the dew on the grass, destiny like the dart of lightning - emptied in an instant, vanished in a flash.

—Dōgen, *Fukanzazengi*

Covid 19 Sutra 1

(early days)

books & blossoms
spring & all
cold morning no
wind cloud bank

over the mountain
ridge city & its
tower in the distance
last night two curious

foxes   young ones
came by for the wild
salmon cooking on
the gas grill

can one be stead
fast now   see
clearly & with
joy at dawn

a male & female
cardinal at the bird
feeder & the red
azaleas blooming along

the fence line
all this before
you check the daily
death count

i am ready
to become something
else   am i
really   dissolve

dissolute   to face
or turn away from
who said ***or*** ?
this is it

& when the virus
hit   can we
change   or does
connection break away

the treasure store
is open you
can take what
you want — no

you can take
what you need
through practice
you may learn

to receive what
is already yours
here is the bell sound
to awaken you

i gave birth
to you   which means
i also gave you
death   & now

my mother   you
find yourself – fever
spiking 104 – in
an ambulance alone

late at night
on the way to
the hospital to
ICU & tests

hard to remain
calm listening to
the death toll
knowing that change

& impermanence
have always been
our nature   but
there is that gap

fear that takes us
far away from
what we think
we know

i think

you are

on your way

& it pains me

that i

that no one

can be

with you

what you are

what you were

dissolving into the virus

at age 89

which is a number
among many other
numbers   your fever
antibodies   the death

count by state
& nation & planet
we study the numbers
& make projections

as the wave
sweeps over us
& some are
swept away

when the Liar attacks
the students of fact
when the Liar says
everything is great

when he is the parasite
arrived before the virus
when he finds enough hosts
to sustain his disease

when he can't find enough
machines to keep us breathing
when he says it every day
with a grin and a shrug

& who

will be

the last person

with you

& who

will be near

but unable

to hold your hand

& who

will tell the story

of what

the numbers mean

what to do

in these perilous

times   he

told me

simply

be as you

are

each breath

continues to take

place in

the fullness

of time

soldier   shoulder
slow words emanate
invasion
of the invisible

"burdens are from God
& shoulders also"
we are becoming
their host

a beautiful spring day
in the moment   nothing changes
in this instant   memory of the dead & dying
to see all beings   as they are   disappearing

my door way is the darkness
i trust the night time
my door way is the early morning
i trust in the light

together we walk
the greening hillside
young dog runs
down   white cows amble

across muddy pasture
above tree line clouds
light darkness   i sit with
a slowly changing cedar tree

yes   i will
go up to
the stars
this language

that we are
goes only so far
in peril
of the invisible

quiet running water
yes
i will go up
to the stars

Covid 19 Sutra 4

(we're back?)

actuality is not
flat   this morning
the voice has not
entered me   shadowy

light through pines
to see it steadily
peace & compassion
are these the voice

it itself remains
the question   head
heart hand   trans
mission is happening

we could think
about it forever
walking upon the bare
ground   i look down

transparent   eyeball
i have no head
i never did
it all passes

through me i am
a door way   a portal
an occasion by which
it arrives

magical catalyst (3 for José Kozer)

read this remember
something else mind
in tranquility sees

it as it
arises it is
place that shelters
you know one

place well changing
light seasonal
dance of green & gold
this happens to you

We debate the meaning of the numbers. (3 for José Kozer)

Infection count, death count, caught in a time delay.

Death of logic, death of rationality, science becomes
something to believe or not.

Once that verb gets introduced, science finds itself cast
into a space where it perishes.

The future has contracted into now & the next few months.

Pileated woodpecker pounds the railing of the deck.

Whoever told you that observing your mind was easy?

I can't live like this all the time.

We already are self-driving cars.

Nothing so pleasing as that first bowel movement of the day.

Hydrangeas are beginning to bloom & a few gardenias too.

Time & change: listen to the tune underneath it all.

(3 for José Kozer)

meaning cannot be
extracted from daily
reality so don't
expect it in a

poem   cascade
of overlapping bird
calls traffic & human
activity mix with

wind through trees
who would seize
on one thing
over another

The visitor insinuates himself among us.

He is not from here not from now, he is not familiar with our ways.

Cast a cold eye on life, cast a cold eye on death, horseman fly by.

It is not exactly how you remember it.

> The visitor cannot understand what we do to one another; he cannot understand why we make such a big deal about our different appearances.
>
> Who can name the trees & birds in your own backyard.
>
> She is very afraid, but she still has a job (& benefits).
>
> We call them "heroes" & "essential" but we will not pay them a living wage nor will we keep them safe.

>> The orange-faced Liar with raccoon eyes says, "vaccine or no vaccine, we're back."
>>
>> Put your thumbs up & honk your horns.
>>
>> Bar graphs & pie charts served daily.
>>
>> Just how much can you stand to know?

we remain a
question to
ourselves
questionable

enigma beings
determined
to know
what being

is   & then
there is this to
deal with   which
is too much to think about

is &

it

gnats

among bigger words

my life or

yours

one among many

destined

to be for

gotten

what is *that*

tapping at the door

it is
his odd
cadence that i
remember

carry forward
or my father's
posture
hand on hip

return to
the breath
which is
everyone's

Beyond the door was much the same.

They had quarantined, they had sheltered in place, & now the door stood open by order of the Liar.

Because it is invisible, because it depends upon the telling of science, many pretended it didn't exist.

Hydrangeas bloom, gardenias too, spring turned humid with afternoon thunderstorms.

Some asked, "who am I," and "what really matters."

Some learned quickly to love the quiet isolation.

Some couldn't stand it, & they beat their wives & children.

The Liar kept naming others to blame for it all.

Predictions varied about what will happen in the fall.

Some got it right, some didn't, some said money & greed would determine the plan.

A million died with no family & no friends at their bedside.

Each community & each state handled it differently: let a million deaths bloom.

an interwoven
tissue   cosmos
existing & pushing
us toward mutual

awareness   through
me & you writing
poems about itself
joy of such moments

arising & dissolving
i love this world
more
than i had thought

It will never be over; it will never go away.

Red-bellied woodpecker & white-breasted nuthatch cling differently to bark of the pine tree.

It is a test of our cleverness; it is a test of our compassion.

The bloom-color depends upon acidity of the soil.

Like grapes, tomatoes have an exactness of taste specific to variety & location.

I retreated from big cities nearly fifty years ago.

Melville's *The Confidence Man* (published on April Fool's Day 1857) foretold it all: the huckster, the salesman, the liar at the heart of American life.

By means of this technology at hand as a group we sit together in silence.

What is there to see, what is there to say, *now* extends its way throughout the universe.

We can't see them but there are plenty of other worlds happening right now.

I am glad that every now & then we can have this conversation.

I still cannot tell you what consciousness is.

there's nothing there

when are you

when called into

being

aware of it

before it all

gets organized

into the already

known cat

at the back door

wants in

you know what to do

"We inherited a broken, terrible system," Trump told reporters on April 18. "Our cupboards were bare. We had very little stockpile."[1]

Branches of the gardenia bush bow down overflowing with blossoms.

"Trump can lie, but the numbers cannot. Obama left office with an unblemished record of building up the nation's pandemic preparedness. Trump systematically sought to dismantle it."[2]

The new sod – centipede – is beginning to take root filling in the bare patches.

"By Obama's final year, the nation's preparedness on all measurements was 98% to 100%. That's by the Trump administration's own assessment."[3]

If it's not possible to sit in the morning, I sit in the afternoon.

"If the cupboard was bare, it's because Trump swept it clean."[4]

Typically drawn in the shape of a quickly & expertly drawn not fully closed zero, the *enso* itself displays a generative emptiness.

"Vaccine or no vaccine, we're back," says Trump. (May 15, 2020)

"He was just in a fucking rage. He was saying, 'This is so unfair to me! Everything was going great. We were cruising to re-election!'"[5]

"American virus deaths at 100,000: What does a number mean?"[6]

"We're back." ? My ass, you stupid motherfucker. As if a cloud came over me…

1 [1]*St. Louis Post-Dispatch*, May 25, 2020.
2 [2] *St. Louis Post-Dispatch*, May 25, 2020.
3 [3] *St. Louis Post-Dispatch*, May 25, 2020.
4 [4] *St. Louis Post-Dispatch*, May 25, 2020.
5 [5] Gabriel Sherman, *Vanity Fair*, May 26, 2020.
6 [6] Associated Press headline, May 27, 2020.

From *field recordings of mind in morning* (2021)

don't lose what is happening to you this morning

they were wanderers out of necessity
my father's parents left Russia
(or is it now Lithuania)
crossed Siberia by train
(ten days i was told)
met up with relatives in Harbin
then moved to Yokohama
& eventually moved to the small farming town of
San José California
where my father was born in 1926

we always lived nearby   within walking distance
& saw them every week   Fanya & Chaim

each had a calmness & steadiness that
they seemed unaware of

some true ancestors we get to know
in the slow practice
of being's unfolding

8/25/19

if it is to greet the dawn
if that is what matters most
if it is a greeting of the light
if that awakening can be carried into the day
if it is as a lantern or candle held in the hand
if the eyes bear witness to the slow
unfolding the subtle caressing of first light
across the hillside & into the pasture
if often i am permitted to return to a meadow
if the light is the light of mind
& the lantern is the word itself first light & first word
quiet & present as the pasture itself
who sees it & walks here with three brown dogs
along the horizon rings the tone of sudden change
this is exactly what happens
as it so happens

9/15/19
Duncan Farm

if one stares back
what of that life
is there

not emotion but
sensation
recollected in
tranquility
when sensation is
precisely what has
disappeared

& tranquility
hardly the case

or these few words
eyes   to mind   to heart

yes   yes   let us
take it all to heart

9/15/19 (2)
Carrollton

some said sorrow
& another said
they are doing a study
& one said it was
fake enthusiasm

it would never be all that much

she was saying
most of it
waving her hands & arms
& the older men at the round table
seemed strangely calm
& one said it was
joyous

"*It still holds joy* is the croaking of frogs.
It still holds consciousness is the singing of earthworms." <629>

4/23/18
New Orleans

"However, now a mountain goat hangs by its horns in emptiness." <634>

as unto calm
as unto death
as that which
you have been
called to know

near full moon
a walk at mid
night with the
youngest dog
a walk upon
the hillside
a walk among shadowy
shapes   a walk
in time   among
glistening figures

4/29/18
Carrollton

time

&

light

& the young cows   peering out at us   curiously
through the barbed wire

“The forest runs around the hunting dog.” <634>

4/29/18

Carrollton

because the bell is
ringing   because
squirrels are at
the bird feeder
because i am already
becoming awake
because each moment
is this moment
because in every moment
there is birth
& death   because
i am nothing more
than a location for change

there is this small opening

it looks like nothing
you have seen before
& it will take you to

other worlds

once across
leave the boat
& go on

it may or

may not

happen right now

"… making a vow to bring all sentient beings [to the shore of enlightenment] before you bring yourself." <655>

6/15/18

the hidden gem
is the light of
morning the hay
baler's row of
yellow discs beside
the giant cedar tree
wild hibiscus
thriving beside the
illuminated farmhouse
gem hidden in
the dreams of the
sleeping woman a
place for *shekinah* to hide
gem hidden with
three brown dogs at
rest after running the
dew covered hillside at
dawn hidden in the
intricate nerves ligaments &
muscles of this illuminated
hand as its writing
opens up
into the light

6/16/18

Duncan Farm   for Joseph Lease

so the trees
speak to
one another
underground &
through the air

& i sit at
daylight after
walking the dogs up
& back down
the hillside

light streams in
through eastern
facing curtains
& i arise

mountains
walk

& the sanskrit word
adhimukti
reaches me

last night
in the warm darkness

sitting beneath

a dome of stars

"At the very moment of sitting, what is sitting?
Is it an acrobat's graceful somersault
or the rapid darting of a fish?" <667>

7/4/18

Duncan Farm

68

"Without reverence, there is no taking refuge." <839>

i had not realized all
along this writing was
moving toward something
perhaps it is an
extended mystical pathway
to be walked only by
one   i had hoped
others would
come along   only
time will tell

11/10/18

walk it with me

it takes time

for the clear words to emerge

walk it with me

“You take refuge in dharma
because it is good medicine.” <840>

11/11/18

de

pends

up

on

so much
depends upon
it all hangs
in the balance

so much so

time of these words
making a place & it all
depends upon your
being here really being
here

"Still, when you clarify that there is nothing to be disliked or longed for, then the original face is revealed by your practice of the way." <877>

what it means depends upon what you think meaning is

12/24/18

for there is the holiness of caring for them

if i am with you
i am with you
here

& when the call comes
from another species

we may call them pets
& say we train them
they are
among our teachers

do you listen
to what
the trees
are saying
underground

"Rejoicing is a gate of realizing dharma;
it keeps the mind calm & at ease." <898>

3/9/19

From *When the Time Comes* (2022)

how lovely is the book
    product of quiet mornings
        product of yes no & maybe

how lovely is the book
    extending hours of grief
        providing clothing for memory

how lovely is the book
    immersed in sorrow & injustice
        refusing all false hope

how lovely is the book
    product of many hands
        community of gathered words

how lovely is the book
    attending to the sound of each syllable
        with its secret music

how lovely is the book
    seeing clearly
        having given up all ideas

how lovely is the book
    uncertain of itself
        until you take it up

how lovely is the book

which you have chosen

& which has chosen you

From “Deathwatch for My Mother, Wendy Lazer”

there it was 4/14/2021
& that is that
a life come down
to amazingly loud

screams yelling
for *mommy* & *daddy*
i want to go home
help help

last resort last
stop on the line
morphine every hour
alternating terror & rest

where is the home
you want to go to i ask
& you say with such
pain *i don't know*

& you say you have seen
an angel in the room
do you know the angel's name
in pain you say *i don't know*

& the angel does not
bring comfort or peace
when the door is open
the entire hall can hear your screams

each day the same
until it isn't
& after that
what is there

that changes
perhaps not
for you
but for us

in adjustments
& surprises of memory
as we find our way
into your state

you grow intimate
with death
which your screams
never address

. . .

the sun is old & mostly 4/17/2021
absent   somewhere outside
it really is spring   you
& your yelling spiral downward

into silence   what is a
breath   taken one at a
time   find it   soon   *hurry*
you will find it

my sister & i   come to be
with you   greet the dawn
with coffee on the balcony
for us   a slow succession of days

your husband   your daughter
your son   each coping
as you are   in an individual
& inward way with your dying

i do not feel whole
without these words
knowing though they are
to you of little use

eyes & shadows   ears
alert & acute   who knows
what is happening
in your scrolling mind

. . .

4/18/2021

gown gloves face shield
& mask   we enter
your room   morphine
klonopin   & another new

anti-psychotic barely touch
you   every five seconds
you croak out a steady
syllable   *ma   ma   ma*

sometimes *help* sometimes
out   my sister & i
encounter a black box
no way to know

what is going on inside
no way to know if
the shouted syllable
carries any meaning

we are told it is a rare
neurological response
perhaps the result of
brain cancer   you do

answer some questions   are you
in pain   *NO*   do you know
we are here   *YES*   then
the return of   *MA   MA   MA*

.   .   .

mind the affectation
mind   pride of knowing &
choosing   you were so
very bright   & you remained

hidden from yourself
mind now stuck on one
syllable   ever
adventurous   you have gone

as far as you can
we wave from the shore
lord of sorrow
compels your simple song

what is that rumbling
i just heard
beside your balcony
coconuts up above ripen slowly

at the top of this palm tree
a local parrot rests briefly
on an extended branch
invisible beginner

you are becoming what is
next   though we
see you   & are with you
we cannot know

. . .

trees stood green 4/21/2021

what did they mean

ma ma ma

said again & again

some hum a song

some sing it to

themselves is there

something underneath

a painful climb

to the end of normal time

being so still

at the root of everything

From "And Then"

1

to the one who died
          love goes by other names
                    an invisible force

underneath each moment
          sits silently
                    beside the one

who is trying to die
          does not judge
                    does not question

opens up at the edge
          of presence
                    in a temporary gown

mask & gloves
          listens to soothing music
                    & reads rotating statements

the unanswered question
          what are you thinking
                    what are you experiencing

there is no big story to tell
        no crashing dramatic moment
                only the slow enigmatic

enclosed present moment
        & minute fractal increments
                of your approach

to something
        we have designated as
                the end

we sit beside
        whatever is happening
                love

presence
        ignorance
                & limitation

intertwined
        we are held here
                beside you

a glimpse
        of the mystery
                all that our eyes can bear

5

haste of words moves across
the slowness of time
one nurse says

you will die very soon
another says stable & unchanged
you gave me this gift

i present it to you
why write a poem   such an
unreasonable thing

because it is what i do
a reckoning   a wreck
beyond which there is no way you

can tell us what is next
words press up to & fog the pane
between us & it

empty form
soon emptied of time
we are wise to you

knowing there is no other way
this impossible spring time
where you live   an island in

perpetual bloom   tropical
remembering too is such a bloom
turned toward another light

suffering too is our communion
we go down with you
for there is no way out

being with you
we are into it
up to a point

dire & extreme
without food or liquid
you cannot move

though you move us
in the screaming of your one syllable
not rage   not disavowal

this enigma   just as anything
resonant & suggestive
of something else

as music sets a mood
    & is also
        simply itself

not in the service of some other
    purpose   your shoulders
        rise & fall with your breathing

i have it in good confidence
    that your pace maker
        will know to stop when you do

may you hear us speaking to you
    let us be with your breath
        that steady rise & fall

From *P I E C E S* (2022)

Shabbat – May 20, 2000

Here's what I did to "prepare" for my first direct conversation with God –

purchase this diary notebook

pick an afternoon time when house empty

create my own "formal" opening statement – (a) the first part of the מה טבו, the lines of beauty said by Balaam, followed by a repetition of (b) ה׳ ה׳

I said the blessing for, & put on my tallit – put on my blue kepah, set the timer for 10 min, walked out on the sun deck, sat down comfortably, set/started the timer, & quietly but audibly talked to God. Time went very quickly

May 22, 2000

Much simpler – same routine to start, dressed informally (no shoes on), again to sun deck, again mid-aft., <u>15</u> min., mainly <u>praising</u> God.

June 6 2000

5:45 AM Awakening. Beautiful early morning sky. I'm restless, anxious – prof. problems c̄ on-going suit. I want to talk to God. Bathrobe on, out to sun-deck, & I talk – the magnificence of it all! Of Creation. The system works! In a crazy way, it's even glorious that I'm being sued, that I'm in danger of losing my malpractise insurance. As the sky lightens further I can see a dizzy-ingly bunch of purple flowers thru a gap in the hedge between the sundeck & the home of George & Marina. I keep praising God, audibly. I feel refreshed.

10.8.2021 / Duncan Farm

how did i

get so lucky

*

& then

there is

the next

moment

*

from 21 years ago

he gave me this gift

of his most intimate

words

a blessing

& a conversation

with god

*

i have

some of her ashes

sitting on

the writing desk

*

her younger brother

& now her

*

head

heart

hand

indeed

what more

might a page

hold

*

three brown dogs

living in

the procession

of time

*

dancing

with integrity &

grace

*

i ask you

as

i ask myself

simply

to listen

*

so

opcn

to it

*

a piece of toast

& some granola

*

all time

before

& after

what i see

*

what to make

of any day

*

“All I knew or know

began with this – <Robert Creeley / *Pieces* p. 58>

emptiness

with its incessant movement.”

*

aggregated

singularity

*

10.9.2021 Duncan Farm

too few words

better than

too many

*

take some portion

of her ashes

make a circle

around the cedar tree

is this what

being becomes

*

once written

i am

no longer here

*

drive

he said

to anyone

who would listen

*

shake it up

baby

twist & shout

*

cloud

cover

*

what words

return

*

in this vein
he made up
a ritual
to communicate
with
god
wrote one page
& left the rest
of this notebook
blank
*
have a piece of toast
with butter
or with jam
*
it simply isn't
the same sky
from day to day
light is time
*
i am up early
& write
until you awaken
*
let this be
a place
for compassion

*

she lives in memory

as do we all

until there is

no one left who remembers

. . .

10.10.2021 /Duncan Farm

what

does it mean

but really

what do you

mean by meaning

*

what

counts

*

you

made it

a ritual

*

minimal

music

ever present

*

say it

to yourself

*

flip

the script

*

which

word

now

*

breathes

through you

so gently

*

what

is

it

. . .

10.27.2021

door

ajar

adore

a jar

*

before
& after
the word
*
the word
made flesh
the word
made fresh
*
plan it
planet
*
conjure man
with his bag
of herbs
& roots
*
bottle
tree
*
oh liberty
what
would you be
now
*
sung
if you sing it

with care

caring

. . .

10.29.2021

it does

get better

*

& it does

get worse

*

a banana

would be good

but we don't

have any bananas

*

i have

no ox to gore

i have

no ax to grind

*

"the death of

one is <Creeley / *A Day Book* / np>

many"

*

i don't have
all my words
in mind
*
calming
slippers

. . .

10.30.2021

what
makes sense
makes sense
because of
the kind of
creature you are
*
brown dog
actively sniffing
everywhere
tracking &
imagining a world
immediately present
& unknown
to you
*

my uncle
in tallit &
blue kepah
called out
to god
that he was
here
henayni
along with lines
of true beauty
*
truth
is to
whom
& what
*
anything seen
in an enlightened manner
becomes revelatory

. . .

11.4.2021 Aptos CA

ghost tree
lone tree
& a redwood's
sense of time

*

humans

too troubled

too busy

for the slowness

syrupy slowness

of being here

in time

*

house lived in

for twenty years

sold

to someone else

*

what

still

hangs in air

invisible texture

memory

& story

long gone

the reasons for anger

*

maybe

it's what they would have done

in the old country

a few jewish families

came over the mountain
from san josé to capitola
to spend a month in the summer
in cottages beside the sea
*
there was the young boy
who took care of
the injured bird –
he had a hawk
but this one was
a cormorant
i think
*
connected senses
making this place
now
& then
*
wait a minute
stunned
by red-tipped
ice plant
in unexpected sunlight

. . .

11.7.2021 Tuscaloosa

i think

i am

awake

*

11.10.2021

tell me

exactly

who or what

is saying

my body

my mind

*

oh

my

morning

light

*

it

takes shape

though i don't know

what it is

until much later

if ever

. . .

11.12.2021

thinking
is the real
dancing its way
inward

. . .

11.24.2021

gold coins
jewels
gems
easy
to carry with you
when it's time
to flee
*
she sewed
one gold coin
into the hem
of her dress
*

how did we

become this

*

if they were

aware

of their awareness

did they

marvel

at it

*

what i

want to know

is

. . .

11.26.2021 Duncan Farm

let us then

together

*

as a child

i had found that place

alone

& totally absorbed

working through

advanced mathematical problems

*

how did his

notebook

come into my possession

*

origin stories

run into

erasure

*

place your bets

& then

the wheel spins

*

i placed a bale of hay

in a field in Alabama

& so location

came to be known

coming & going

from such a port

*

what's

on your mind

make

something up

*

of asterisk

i sing to you

*

morning happens

moon still there

cold november breeze

trees nearly bare

eyes upon the shadows

dogs across the pasture

*

he needed to do it

this way:

early morning

from the sun deck

"mainly *praising* God"

. . .

12.4.2021

i was not asleep

it happened

in the waking world

*

one question

& then

another

*

12.6.2021

sitting
being
of the space
within which
questions
arise
*
though studied & discussed
as nouns
being
& time
turn out to be verbs
holding still
i witness their unfolding
which is
what i am doing too
*
clarity of mind
seeing itself
changing

. . .

12.11.2021

stories

expand

& contract

just like breathing

. . .

12.18.2021

placed

here

to see

& say

*

how consciousness

manages

to float out

into the world

*

he said

world, world –

the miracle

that there is

something to stand on

*

displacing

the tiny self

its worries & concerns

*

with awakened awareness

it might be sun

it might be rain

. . .

12.22.2021

transmission

occurs

when you sit

transmission

takes place

when you sit

*

he walked out quietly

onto the sundeck

gathering the silence about him

before he began to speak

*

who will know it

21 years from now

*

who

is entitled

to such mysticism

*

just as there had been

water on other planets

thousands & thousands

of years ago

*

he was tired

of reading about it

tired of studying

what they had experienced

*

"& a dull person

is good <Suzuki / *Sandokai* / 41>

because he is dull"

*

they say

the mind

making connections

& then

it is sunrise

*

the sun

is but a morning star

he saw it so

& then again

so did he

*

at first-hand

which means

that you can

& must

do it too

*

second

after second

we used to say

the clock is ticking

*

do you read me

roger

over

& out

*

he is waiting still

on the sundeck

listening

waiting for an answer

here we are

waiting with him

From *As We Vanish from Public View* (2024)

the famed director
called it nature deficit disorder
there are millions unknowing
night sky & the language of trees

underground & through the air
we walk between dis
tracted defended against
this miraculous happening

time
takes us down one at a
time
earth

is the bardo
a paradise for
getting soul in
scribed for its return

alive at that time
i hold the book
capacious brain
raining down its chosen rhapsody

4.3.2023 (2) / Duncan Farm

if
it
were to
be
as
this

one
by
one

within
this shining
life

sing it
so
the moment

resounds
joy
of each
& each
& every
because
you entered
in

incarnate
instance
of meat
& bone

location
for ongoing
change

if it were
to be as
this

4.22.2023
Notre Dame

a vine

wraps its way

up

a tree trunk

*

to my dog

Nate

as he is finishing

a seizure

i repeat

i am with you

*

as over

flow

he said

& meant

abundant life

5.2 & 4. 2023

don't try

to do

too much

how does

the goldfinch

manage

transformation

will it rain

this morning

i remember her

by holding

her ashes

by giving them up

to the ground

japanese maple

aflame in late

light

how do you see it

taking notice

emptying your

self

the goldfinch

& the rose-breasted

grosbeak

5.5.2023 (2)

if the chimney
if the flesh
if the diagnosis
if the time he has
left
if the body responds
more slowly
if the pair of pileated
woodpeckers together
hammer the wood railing
if the morning
brings surprising moisture
if her voice
can only be imagined
if recollection or
the language of the crows
is somehow not enough
if the ferns gardenias &
wild roses have made it
to return & the deer
bed down in nearby woods
if there are no clouds
if her ashes
sit on a shelf
above my books

5.28.2023

their nursery

        & ours

born

        out of darkness

bright fire

        raging in the void

a constellation

        or a human relationship

happening

        with the exactness of lightning

or a

        contagious music

those sudden

        one-second dreams

because you had been

        reaching out

it was what

        was given to you

you were being

held carefully

6.25.2023 (2) / Duncan Farm / lightning storm 11:15pm

oh
so this
is what i see
self dissolving
by means of
aging or
practiced attention
woven into
fabric of tree
hillside &
pasture a
moment in
which something
has broken
open

8.21.2023 / Duncan Farm

fact is

the sadness

of it all

could kill you

i have it

on good faith

the dog at my feet

chewing on a bone

will die as

will i

though who knows

who goes first

my neighbor & i

walk along

the dirt road past

the hay barn

we wonder who put out

the poison for coyotes

when the poison

killed another neighbor's

three dogs

fact is sadness

turns to prayer

fact is prayer

turns to song

9.4.2023 / Duncan Farm

do i

    or does the mind

i have been

    given

behave the way

    clouds do

such is time

    by day & night

i live as a friend

    intimate

with the invisible

    so do you

where is the sound

    of these words

as you hear them

    for yourself

sun behind

    the cedar tree

shadows stretched across

    dew-covered hillside

dirt road

    stays in place

9.11.2023 / Duncan Farm

what do you call it

step away

he slept through the night

& into the morning

without a seizure

leaves turn yellow &

pine needles rain down

half moon overhead

you are always somewhere

as is my cousin Ben

as is my sister Terri

what of the treasured

& remembered dead

beginning with father

& mother   where

now returned to

faces before birth

memory too

has its seasons

who do you

recall as trees

shed their leaves

long ago he chose

to live in the woods

what happened to the books

& all they pointed toward

you are here to pass

on what comes to mind

11.4.2023

somewhere head, perhaps <CA, 71>

within gray

day without dawn

dry golden

hillside above the pasture

mind imposture

& a quiet being

isn't it all

ontological

what to study

when not knowing

is most intimate

& this

his last words

head perhaps

a rest

within a mystery

called time

& you are

always somewhere

for Charles Alexander

11.12.23 / Duncan Farm

up the ladder

    to the home

not this house

    but another

never more than

    this   first

winter-like day

    sunrise &

steam rising from

    golden brown grass

dormant as in

    who is yet

to awaken

    articles vanish

invisible subatomic

    particles dance about

evading our crude

    detection   up

the ladder to

    a hidden house

11.23.2023 / Thanksgiving / Duncan Farm

what he shot

he dragged back

to the house

to cure

said green meat

is the worst

part &

parcel

the gift i

carry with me

a word

might bring it

to a boil

in sight

of a path

to the afterlife

what you had
            seen & been
vanished within
            your forgetting

i don't outlive
            my sorrow i
am with it

floating island
            a word
adrift

is there ever
    enough
of being here

to notice
    & to thank

11.25-26.2023 / Duncan Farm

New Poems

Chaim's Letters, 1971-72

yes
this is it

somehow
i found a
stack of letters
he had sent me
in 1971 & 1972
after i had moved
to Virginia

my father's father
was quiet
humble &
deferential
though he
had his opinions

i was very smart
or so i thought
& that
caused plenty
of problems

my grandfather
Chaim
had left
Russia
or was it
really Lithuania
or Ukraine
as a young man
living in Harbin
& then Yokohama
before settling in
San Jose

fluent in Hebrew
Yiddish Russian
& English
he owned & ran
Lazer's Market
a small grocery store
on San Jose's east side

he wrote to me
with such gratitude
& patience
confused by the violence
& impatience of my generation's
call for a new

American revolution
it took longer
to write a letter
than a poem
& the letters
took a few days
to arrive
long distance phone calls
were too expensive
for us to afford

his tiny determined
scrawl reached me
every few weeks
full of questions
& observations

as I read the letters now
fifty years later
i can begin to infer
who i was

Lao Tzu asks
"if you aren't free of yourself
how will you ever become yourself"
in 1971 i was
full of myself

unable to forget myself
so that now
a few years older
than Chaim was at
his death
i can sit in a chair
quietly
as he did

approaching his own
death
he did not discuss it

he wrote again & again
doubting the actual
existence of Jesus
& even if Jesus did
walk the earth
he insisted
when the messiah arrived
there should have been
peace

Chaim truly mourned
that a peace-loving humanity
had not occurred
his pain & disappointment

registered in every letter
i wrote him back
every month
as i am doing now

to be specific
he wrote on March 18 1972
"Common sense tells us
that peace is the best choice –
but how long does it have to take
to bring it to a reality?
I don't give up hope
but have no definite date."

did i know
any better then
do i now
as the disappointment
& human failings now
seem so much greater

his family lived
"on the Lithuanian
and Russian border"
& he left at the age
of conscription
"sure to be inducted
in a month or so."

at night he could
hear the artillery

"my mother was just as much [as]
I opposed to help in this war
waged by a country mistreating us
one who had
nothing but contempt [for] us."

"It was easy to decide
where to go. We had
relations in N. Y.
and could expect some help."

he wrote to remind me
we are a people
of the book

i was pursuing a Ph.D.
in literature
& it has taken me
all these intervening years
to figure out which books
& which words

in the book i am
reading now
a woman who just turned 80

& is approaching her own death
has the patience & clarity
& common sense of my grandfather

she begins each day by saying
"I vow to be grateful for this precious
human birth.
I vow to be present.
This is it."

Chaim
who was i
you were writing to

i am present now
reading his letters
from 50 years ago
as i sit quietly
in an old farmhouse
looking out at a cedar tree
where i have
scattered some of
my father's & mother's
ashes

1.21.2023 / Duncan Farm

Duncan Farm November Meditation

1

what died with father
what died with mother
there was more i wanted to know
say again the names of distant places
russia   lithuania   ukraine
harbin   yokohama   san jose
tell it all now
invisible as you are
there was more
i wanted to hear
you are not your body
you are not your mind
who were you
& where do we come from

2

one by one
they go away

mystery repeats itself

the equal loneliness
of each soul
                              here   & there

3

small dance of wind
from cedar to oak

mind   & its own instants
this

is called thinking
sometimes

at play sometimes
answering to

an invisible
summoning

small dance of wind
beginning
with a distant
pine

4

wild   wildly disordered as it happens   clouds   moment twisted disappearing chronology
of a human life ample in complexity beyond any telling of it

why not a tree's or a dog's experience of time

what lies beyond the limits of our attention

sit with eyes open wide

5

who is with you

from all that was

6

piety kept quiet

& the clouds were revelation

this

is where it all appears

because

nothing in the whole world

is hidden

later that night he found

skunks
in the hay barn

yes
turn the light inward

7

he had the fire then & hardly anyone noticed that is the nature of this exacting path so as you go it will shape you as needed along the way self-pity & disappointment burn away

hold the ember dear it is the given gem

8

farm at night
thin line
of dim light
along the horizon
like the implicit
gap between
blocks of color
in a Rothko painting
my oldest boykin Walt

buried nearby up the way
this morning halfway
up the hillside
just beyond
the cedar tree i find
a large silver wrench
some words
have nothing to do
with our five
or six senses

9

in & out of morning

clouds

i sit in the cross-hairs
of the window pane

10

his joy
was more than others
could accept

so too his sorrow

soon
it
will be light

each
has an instrument
idiosyncratic
played
or simply listened to

be still
& listen

blessed are
　　the pure
in heart
　　for they
are seeking
　　a blessing

awe
　　surrounds us
in all
　　that is

to see God
　　the light
too bright
　　& all
gone dark

& the darkness
　　becoming
stars &
　　constellations

synapses
　　of being
& being
　　seen

forms
    incarnate
& a brief flickering
    of consciousness
momentary
    partial
& impermanent

blessed
    are the pure
who cannot
    endure

the word
    & the way
swaying
    like branches
on a summer
    tree

1.8.24 / Duncan Farm

something is happening

like in the old days
        awakened at dawn
by a compelling
        flash of language
because you know
        something is happening
but you don't know
        what it is
did i spend my life
        collecting old
soda pop bottles or head vases
        i happened upon
many books of poetry &
        i saved them
& i wrote some myself
        to whom
does it matter now
        there was a young singer
with a sharp accusing voice
        & he was a door way
& a flash of light

so you know
        something is happening

& you don't know
            what it is
the voice persists
            beyond the burning
of the books
            beginning of the end game
a foggy february morning
            wife son & dog
sleeping in
            world gone mad
in sadly astonishing ways
            & you know
something is happening
            but you don't know
what it is
            for the body you inhabit
is it the dawning
            of a cancer or a tumor
or simply a spell
            of not feeling well

fog among the stand
            of pine trees
no birds or squirrels
            at the feeders
scratching of a fine point pen
            across a lovely white page

we did these things

as beckoned

is this the time

of dying i

have come upon

to whom

can it be told

fog sinking in

among the pines

& the wrought iron

gateway

2.1.2024

the japanese maple
  inserts
itself into the spring
  conversation
start
  doing something
his mother told him
  to make something
of himself
  with his father
who seldom spoke
  except to
tell long jokes
  it was
implied
  years later
april sixth
  trees leafing
their initial yellowy green
  azaleas popping
pink white & red
  blooms
soon the indigo bunting
  will be a shimmery blue
what is your
  instrument

4.6.2024

NOTES

The Notes are primarily condensed versions of more extensive notes or After Words that appear at the back of most of my published books.

My deepest thanks to the editors/publishers of the fourteen books from which *Abundant Life: New & Selected Poems* has been chosen. *Days.* New Orleans: Lavender Ink, 2002 [Bill Lavender]; *Elegies & Vacations.* Cambridge, UK: Salt Publishing, 2004 [Chris Hamilton-Emery]; *The New Spirit.* San Diego: Singing Horse Press, 2005 [Paul Naylor]; *Portions.* New Orleans: Lavender Ink, 2009 [Bill Lavender]; *N18 (Complete).* San Diego: Singing Horse Press, 2012 [Paul Naylor]; *Poems Hidden in Plain View,* PURH: Presses universitaires de Rouen et du Havre, 2016 [Christophe Lamiot Enos]; *Thinking in Jewish (N20).* New Orleans: Lavender Ink, 2017 [Bill Lavender]; *Evidence of Being Here: Beginning in Havana (N27).* Mobile, Alabama: Negative Capability Press, 2018 [Sue Walker]; *Slowly Becoming Awake (N32),* Loveland, Ohio: Dos Madres Press, 2019 [Robert Murphy]; *Poems That Look Just Like Poems,* PURH: Presses universitaires de Rouen et du Havre, 2019 [Christophe Lamiot Enos]; *COVID 19 SUTRAS.* New Orleans: Lavender Ink, 2020 [Bill Lavender]; *field recordings of mind in morning*. Buffalo, NY: BlazeVOX, 2021 [Geoffrey Gatza]; *When the Time Comes.* Loveland, Ohio: Dos Madres Press, 2022 [Robert Murphy]; *P I E C E S.* Buffalo, NY: BlazeVOX, 2022 [Geoffrey Gatza]. And in the New Poems section, thanks to Lou Rowan, *Golden Handcuffs Review,* and Ron Slate, *On the Seawall,* for publishing new poems.

Thanks to Joseph Lease for help and advice in making the selections for this book, and for his friendship. Thanks to Charles Alexander for layout & design, and for his many years of friendship.

Days

Days was a joyous experiment (1994-95) – the opening of a door or a way to write that has remained with me ever since. As I began to conceive of *Days,* I felt pulled again in the direction of a more lyrical poetry, and I wanted to examine the resources of the short line. As I wrote these poems, their daily quality became crucial: assessing and accounting for, reflecting and making and remarking upon the minute variations of each day. The series of poems also required that I think about the inherent conflict between the selectivity and intensified focus of the lyrical as opposed to the less decisive, unremarkable gradations of the daily. I soon settled on the framework of a year's writing project, which I finally revised to a year-and-a-day.

Days allowed me a means to return to a musicality and lyricism that felt very joyous—a way away from some of the implicit do's and don't's of avant garde praxis; a means back into modes of beauty that I had (perhaps mistakenly) abandoned. The tutelage of Thelonious Monk, I hope, kept the writing "wrong" enough to stay fresh, shifting quickly enough to remain of interest.

Elegies & Vacations

Elegies & Vacations includes poems that are at once elegiac, skeptical, and spiritual. At the heart of the book is a long poem, "Deathwatch for My Father," which tracks my father's final months, testing out the capacities of innovative poetry in the face of the death of a loved one. The book explores relationships with the dead—from my father, to John Cage, to George Oppen—while also projecting forward to ask "to what are we ancestral."

The New Spirit

While *Days* explored the lyrical or musical possibilities of a brief poem, *The New Spirit* extends that musicality into a suite-like composition, guided by my long-term engagement with John Coltrane's *A Love Supreme.*

Portions

I began writing *Portions* on May 29, 2001. *Portions* constituted my next phase of writing after completing *The New Spirit*. It took me quite some time (nearly eighteen months) to come up with a form that engaged me enough to work with it over a substantial period of time. Initially the form of *Portions,* due to the very short lines, made me think more fully about the multiple possibilities of line breaks – the way the line break offers both a discontinuity and a space through which one reads to connect. In some ways, the condensed form allowed me to explore the quick compression, turns, and fusion that I found in Celan's poetry. While some of the lyrical pleasures of *Days* can also be found in *Portions,* the latter has less of an insistence upon melopoeia or traditional modes of lyricism, and, at times, works more deliberately with possibilities of statement or returns (as in my first poems) to the resources of anecdote and narrative. Along the way, I encountered a note on form (in Rodger Kamenetz's *Stalking Elijah,* p. 353) of particular pertinence to *Portions*:

> *parashah (pl. parashiot)*: The portion of Torah read on a particular Sabbath. There are 54 portions (sometimes two are combined). Each *parashah* is named for its opening word or first distinguishing word. (cf. parshat *lekh lekha* – Genesis 12:1-17:27)

My form for each poem became 3 X 18 = 54 words, the building block of 18 being a mystical Jewish number. I followed the Torah-portion mode of naming by picking a key word as the title for each poem.

N18 (Complete)

After spending the prior six years writing the poems for *Portions* – all written in an invented fifty-four word form – I craved to work in a more malleable form, and I determined that the *Notebooks* would adhere to the principle that each page would look very different than the previous page. N18 (the eighteenth in my ongoing Notebooks) is the first published full notebook of my shape-writing and includes all pages of Notebook 18.

In *N18*, for the most part I was occupied with reading Levinas' *Otherwise Than Being* and *God, Death, and Time*. As for how I read Levinas, I was not interpreting what I read; it was a productive ongoing adjacency. I channeled key passages from my immediate reading as I was writing. I was often struck by the coincidental confluence of interests between what "I" wrote and what Levinas I read.

Absolutely crucial to the composition (and ethics) of the Notebooks is a complete commitment to the page as a one-time improvisation – a highly focused composition in real time, without drafts or rewrites. Typically, I "see" the page – the shape of the writing – and then I begin writing. Admittedly, there is a naïve quality to these handwritten pages – perhaps something akin to the outsider or folk art so much a part of the culture where I live (in Alabama).

I've come to think of this shape-writing as displaying a kind of vectored thinking. The page becomes the site for the collision of non-cumulative, often conflicting or conflicted, non-sequential thinking. The page is the locale – a non-repeatable, concentrated improvisational duration – for indications of strings of words (truly vectors of force, or lines/ phrases of energy) contending for a place to be seen/heard.

Poems Hidden in Plain View

Poems Hidden in Plain View is a reading of and selection from the first ten notebooks of my Notebooks project. The first ten notebooks led me toward what I now refer to as *shape-writing* – one-time improvisatory compositions in abstract shapes. In part, re-reading and residing in PHPV is my attempt to understand the genesis and nature of shape-writing. Indeed, I was quite surprised to find so very little of it in notebooks one through ten, where, instead of the more radical shape-writing, the difference in appearance from page to page arises from stanzaic variation and shifting word placement, but these notebook pages (for the most part) are relatively rigid with respect to horizontal and vertical axes. Even though shape-writing as a consistent (and consistently variable) mode of composition does not really emerge fully until notebooks eleven through twenty, the writing in notebooks one through ten marks a similar commitment to the page as a one-time improvisation – a highly focused composition in real time, without drafts or rewrites. Perhaps it makes sense to think of notebooks one through ten as prefatory, as the discovery, slowly, of methodologies, processes, and proximities that would allow for a new kind of writing in subsequent notebooks. An important strand of thinking in these notebooks comes from my increasing engagement with my ever-changing understanding of what it means to be a Jew. (Please see the After Words in *Poems Hidden in Plain View* for a discussion of my relationship to Heidegger's writing, particularly *Being & Time*, the book that I was reading as I wrote Notebooks 1-10.)

Thinking in Jewish (N20)

It seems that I thought that this would be the final notebook – the first ten written within a reading of Heidegger's *Being and Time*, and the next ten notebooks (perhaps a balancing out?) written while reading books by Emmanuel Levinas. (Notebooks 1-10 being H [Heidegger]; 11-20 being L [Levinas]; thus, my own initials, HL.) The specific Levinas books that I was reading while writing *N20* were *Of God Who Comes to Mind* and *Entre Nous*. *Thinking in Jewish (N20)* is an odd fusion of various kinds of diaries, journals, and day books, with similar qualities of daily observation, though the Notebooks (not just *N20*) demonstrate a devotion to making manifest intervals of consciousness and occasions of shape-as-momentary-insight.

As for the book's title – *Thinking in Jewish* – a tip of the hat to Jonathan Boyarin who wrote a book of the same title (1996, University of Chicago Press), especially Boyarin's affirmation of what he refers to as his still-unsettled articulation of his own attachment to the name "Jew" (173) and his observation that "what a Jew writes – particularly in a non-Jewish language – is Jewish and non-Jewish at the same time" (195). Mine is a non-essentialized version of being Jewish and thinking in Jewish. The Notebooks are a way of proceeding that is somewhat destabilized, ambiguous, polyvocal, and multi-textual. I agree wholeheartedly with Boyarin's suggestions that "Jewish identity is indeed marked by a constant tension between self-identification, and identification by and as the Other" (112-113). Though clearly not exclusively a Jewish perspective or affinity, *N20* explores what it means to be of the book, and of the word.

Evidence of Being Here (N27)

The 27th Notebook continues and sustains a writing project that began on October 8, 2006. As with Notebooks 21-30, the reading accompanying my writing is from Maurice Merleau-Ponty – in the case of *N27* specifically that great book *Phenomenology of Perception*. "to what degree are we here now   you & i   & in what senses" constitutes perhaps the central questioning of *N27*.

N27 begins with a fourth trip to Cuba, with soprano saxophonist/composer Andrew Raffo Dewar, as we attempted to rectify an earlier experience where our jazz-poetry performance had to be cancelled due to pressure applied by the state (Cuba). On this return trip, we were able to do two public performances, the latter with good friend Omar Pérez (poet, musician, artist, translator) who played percussion (on a handmade cajón). This trip to Cuba also marked our last meeting with the great poet Juan Carlos

Flores, whom I had met several years earlier in Alamar, a Havana suburb, and with whom we had rehearsed and improvised (at his Alamar apartment) a couple of years earlier when Juan Carlos was much healthier. This visit, we met a spectral figure, a man who no longer had a home and who wandered around smoking cigarettes and occasionally eating. The ghostly Juan Carlos whom we met – sunken eyes, strange pronouncements – asked us which was more important, what you know or what you don't know. A year later, Juan Carlos committed suicide.

Slowly Becoming Awake (N32)

This book would not have had typed transcriptions if not for Robert Murphy's (the publisher's) request that I consider doing so. He indicated that he understood that I would probably consider the suggestion somewhat heretical, shape-writing being linked to an intentional slowing down of reading combined with a different physicality of reading (by having to rotate the page frequently in order to continue reading at all). Also, there is something about the shape-writing poem that suggests the motion or dance of thinking itself, perhaps an echo of the dance of synapses throughout some region of the brain.

Initially, I did not like the idea, having clung to a sense that "the whole point" of shape-writing was to create a productive difficulty of reading. But just after I got Robert's email, and before I had time to reply, I went to the Bay Area, mainly to spend time with a master teacher at the Berkeley Zen Center who would help me learn to sew in order to make the *rakusu* (a small but complex bib-like garment – part of lay ordination – that has a very complicated, patchwork way of being sewn). Gradually, over a period of two weeks, I felt my mind changing. Though I spent no time directly thinking about it, as my mind (unpredictable as it is) returned to Robert's suggestion, I found myself shifting slowly from resistance to fascination to happy anticipation. Once I began transcribing the poems, I realized that the transcriptions, like the sewing, had a meditative quality to them, allowing me to re-enter the space of the poem's making with a re-energized fresh reading of each page. The transcription process allowed me once again (somehow) to become a beginner with each page. A second and engaging *now* taking place. It gave me a chance to perform each page in a new way – much as I do when I perform pages from the notebooks in improvisations with jazz musicians.

As with all of my Notebooks, there is an accompanying ongoing reading which for nearly every page becomes a quoted presence along with "my" shape-writing. For *Slowly Becoming Awake (N32)*, the textual dance partner is Dogen's *Shobo Genzo (Treasury of the True Dharma Eye: Zen Master Dogen's Shobo Genzo,* edited by Kazuaki Tanahashi [Shambhala, 2013]), the writing of the 13th century Zen master (1200-1253) who was the founder of Zen's Soto school.

Poems That Look Just Like Poems

Beginning with Notebook 28, I found myself writing poems that were once again – as in some of my work prior to the Notebooks – left-margin justified, and in a language and rhetoric similar to poems that I had written many years ago. For some time, I found this return to a prior conception of the poem somewhat embarrassing – not at all what I imagined or hoped or expected to be writing. At times, these poems struck me as too didactic for my taste. Nonetheless, these poems presented themselves (wrote themselves) with an urgency, clarity, and (eventually) joy that made it impossible not to write them, though they clearly disturbed my sense of what the Notebooks would be. I began to wonder that perhaps in Notebooks 28-31 there may well be quite a few such poems, and that perhaps a book had been (unknown to me) writing itself in this throwback mode. Indeed, that turned out to be the case, and the writing that I initially somewhat jokingly called *Poems That Look Just Like Poems* now inhabits that name quite comfortably.

COVID19 SUTRAS (March 1, 2020 – June 13, 2020)

Writing within the tradition of wisdom literature, *COVID19 SUTRAS* presents a real-time engagement with the early phases of the pandemic, as that tragedy began to merge with the consequences of the death of George Floyd, Black Lives Matter, police brutality, and the increased awareness of the virus of American systemic racism. These poems hold outrage and peace, anger, and momentary joy within a shared space. In the tradition of Chinese poet Tu Fu, the writing anchors itself in a path of sustained Zen meditation and pastoral rejuvenation as means toward balance and insight.

field recordings   of mind   in morning

For me, this is one of the great joys of writing: that we can be doing one thing, with full intent and deep engagement, and yet something else entirely different may be taking place without the writer having the least awareness of it. Perhaps, at times, shape-writing for me had been, unbeknownst to me, simply a way to get the writing done initially. Perhaps it was a disguise and a release, a necessary way of keeping my vision & mind off to the side of what I was doing.

This notion of unraveling – or, of re-figuring the nature of the initial shape-writing – intrigued me enough to look at a prior notebook (#33, written 4/8/18-3/9/19) to see what the prospects might be for harvesting those writings. In unraveling Notebook #33, I have had the added pleasure of re-visiting the passages (one per page) of quoted material. As with *Slowly Becoming Awake (N32)*, the quotations throughout Notebook #33 are taken from my reading of Eihei Dogen's *Shobo Genzo (Treasury of the True Dharma Eye)*, a collection of essays by the 13th century Zen Buddhist who was the founder of Zen's Soto school. Quotation has and continues to be an essential part of my practice of poetry (beginning in 1971 with my engagement with Thoreau's *Journal*).

My writing has been proliferating in ways that I never had imagined. The shape-writing – particularly as manifest in *Slowly Becoming Awake* – has led to improvisational music-poetry collaborations, recordings, and performances. *Thinking in Jewish (N20)* led to two memorable performances with legendary Birmingham guitarist Davey Williams. *Evidence of Being Here: Beginning in Havana (N27)* offered scores (or performance suggestions) for several concerts (in Athens, Georgia and in Havana, Cuba with composer/soprano saxophonist Andrew Raffo Dewar. *Slowly Becoming Awake* became material for a range of different musical performances, from a full choir concert (under the direction of Andrew Minear) to more intimate house concerts with percussionist Justin Greene, flute player Nathaniel Trost, and saxophonist Trygve Seim. More recently, recordings and performances with composer/musician Holland Hopson on banjo.

Field recordings is part of an ongoing exploration of the similarities of meditation (zazen) and the writing of a kind of spontaneous, improvisatory, immediate poetry – a writing of the moment, of specific instants of (morning) consciousness.

When the Time Comes

Detailed observations of the last weeks of my mother's life in an attempt to embrace and be with the mystery and difficulties of her dying. The poems tell portions of my mother's richly active 90 years of life, though my primary attention is to the specific circumstances of her dying, especially the enigmatic syllable that my mother kept repeating. The initial long poem, "Deathwatch for My Mother, Wendy Lazer," takes its place beside the long poem, "Deathwatch for My Father," that I wrote during the final months of my father's life in 1995-96.

PIECES

I have no recollection of how or when I received the beautiful brown leather-bound notebook in which this book was written. *P I E C E S* is at once a book-length meditation in brief fragments and a response to the first page (included here) that had already been written in the found notebook. That first page describes a ritual for speaking to God; it was written by my uncle, Stan Goodman, neurosurgeon and Biblical scholar. *P I E C E S*, in part an homage to Robert Creeley's short-line poems, extends my ongoing development of a new spiritual poetry, continuing the discoveries and questions found in my earlier books, especially *The New Spirit, Poems that Look Just Like Poems,* and *field recordings of mind in morning.*

As We Vanish from Public View

Because that is what is happening now… Poems primarily meditative, seeking momentary and sustaining balance, attentiveness, compassion, and calm, written April-November 2023. Published in 2024 by 7 Points Press, a new small press in Florence, Alabama.

About the Author

Hank Lazer has published thirty-five books of poetry, including his most recent, *As We Vanish from Public View* (7 Points Press) and *field recordings   of mind   in morning* (with 15 music-poetry tracks with Holland Hopson on banjo – available on YouTube). Along with *Abundant Life: New & Selected Poems,* Lazer has published a companion volume of essays, poetics, and interviews: *What Were You Thinking: Essays 2006–2024* (Lavender Ink).
In April 2015, Lazer was selected for the state of Alabama's highest literary award, the Harper Lee Award, for a lifetime of achievement in literature.

Over the past fifteen years, Lazer has collaborated with a range of musicians including Holland Hopson, Davey Williams, Andrew Raffo Dewar, and Jake Berry for poetry-music performances, recordings, and improvisations. He has exhibited a series of video installations of his *Brush Mind* books.

In January 2014, Lazer retired from the University of Alabama (where he continues to teach innovative seminars on Zen Buddhism and Radical Approaches to the Arts for the Blount Scholars Program and OLLI) after 37 years in a variety of positions, including Associate Provost for Academic Affairs, Executive Director of Creative Campus, and Professor of English.

To order books, learn about talks, readings, and workshops, and see photos of Duncan Farm see Lazer's website: https://www.hanklazer.com

About Chax

Founded in 1984 in Tucson, Arizona, Chax has published more than 250 books in a variety of formats, including hand printed letterpress books and chapbooks, hybrid chapbooks, book arts editions, and trade paperback editions such as the book you are holding. From August 2014 until July 2018 Chax Press resided in the University of Houston-Victoria Downtown Center for the Arts. Chax is a nonprofit 501c3 organization which depends on suppport from various government & private funders, and, primarly, from individual donors and readers. In July 2018 Chax Press returned to Tucson. In 2021, Chax Press founder and director Charles Alexander was awarded the Lord Nose Award for lifetime achievement in literary publishing. In January 2024 Chax established a new studio for its letterpress printing and book arts work, and in December 2024 is opening a new public Poetry Reading Room, to be open by appointment and subscription, to showcase books by local presses (including Chax), books by Chax authors, and selected titles of poetry of the past.

Chax Press stands against all attacks on democracy, civil rights, and the dignity and self-determination of all peoples, in the USA and internationally. We stand against authoritarian government, including that which exists within supposedly democratic systems. We stand against all genocides. We stand for equal human rights for all, and we encourage and believe in peace and love as critical to solving problems in our world.

Our current mailing address is 6181 East 4th Street, Tucson, Arizona 85711-1613.
You can email us at *chaxpress@chax.org*

Your support of our projects as a reader, and as a benefactor, is much appreciated.

Find CHAX online at *https://chax.org*

This book has been designed by Charles Alexander, with the assistance of Hank Lazer. Printing services by IPG (Independent Publishers Group).

The font used is Albertina Pro.

www.ingramcontent.com/pod-product-compliance
Lightning Source LLC
LaVergne TN
LVHW070211110826
845147LV00003B/558

* 9 7 8 1 9 4 6 1 0 4 5 7 1 *